IT
ROCKET
SCIENCE

C000097933

THE STRESS-FREE BLUEPRINT
TO A MULTI-MILLION POUND
DENTAL PRACTICE

DR GRANT MCAREE
BDS BSC (HONS)

CONTENTS

'*Parents are the bones on which children sharpen their teeth.*'
Peter Ustinov

This book is dedicated to my parents – Jean and
Ernie McAree – without whom dentistry would not be
a part of my life.

This book is for

Hard-working, stressed-out dentists who want business to be easier and more profitable but are struggling with juggling running a complex business and seeing patients and having some sort of work-life balance.

- Are you a dentist wanting to run an effective dental business?

- Are you someone who wants to open a squat practice?

- Do you feel that the business is solely dependent on your turnover, and this causes immense pressure and unwanted stress on your daily life?

- Is people management sucking your energy?

- Are you struggling to work out what marketing strategy will stop you losing business to the competition?

- If you're honest, is your current work situation affecting your physical health? Maybe causing a bad back and sore neck? And, if you're really honest, is it affecting your mental health too?

- Do you ever feel like packing in dentistry but have nowhere to go?

- Do you feel the pressure from social media posted by colleagues displaying their success, happiness, and perfect lives?

- Do you feel you could lose your job at any time with poor support from your indemnity and a highly regulated system?

Change is always frightening, but it is possible. If any of the above points resonate with you, don't worry; I've helped hundreds of dentists in the same situation and I can show you a way through this.

The life of a dentist can be beautiful. It can be inspiring, to heal the sick and in the process create a masterpiece. To carve a filling that has the same anatomical features as nature intended. It is a job that takes you to the crest of a wave yet has the power to drop you to the depths of hell in an instant.

One of the most stressful of all the medical professions, dentistry is highly regulated and threats of litigation are commonplace. We also have high rates of suicide, divorce, depression and addiction.

So, who the hell would want to be a dentist?

I would!

This book will

Show you how to make running and growing your dental practice easier, smoother and more profitable.

I'll show you how to look at the whole business like a living organism, a tree. We'll take it branch by branch and I'll show you exactly how to get everything running optimally, not just to make more money but so that staff and patients enjoy the time they spend in your practice a hell of a lot more. Once you have the machine smoothly ticking away, you'll feel a lot more in control, relaxed and able to actually switch off and have some down time (remember that?) during evenings and weekends.

I will share how I have seen and done it. All the tips and tricks and knowledge I have gained over a 20-year career dedicated to the building of squat practices. By the time you have finished this book, you will be able to see where your business could do better and exactly what you need to do to change it.

When it boils down to it, your health is the most important of all. You will be able to take back control of your expenses and your business. You will be able to assess your marketing team, your staff and your business as a whole. You will be able to rediscover your passion and love for the job.

As dentists, we are all guilty of having our heads down in the mouth for too many hours. It is a struggle to look up and see what is going on around us. This book will show you there is a way to do both: run an amazing business worth millions and also be able to get on with what you love doing – dentistry!

As you go through this book, I will teach you a totally revolutionary way of running your dental business through tips and tricks that have been tried and tested over many years. It will also show you how to assess your entire patient journey and ensure the team are totally accountable for their actions.

Once you've learned my tips and tricks and used the STFD (Strategy Tree For Dentists) as advised business plan, you will be able to:

- increase revenue

- achieve financial stability

- run your business more effectively by making good decisions with confidence

- confidently sell private treatments

- improve clinical conversion skills

- be less stressed, improving your mental and physical health

- feel less isolated, and surround yourself with people you can trust

- have more time to work on the business

- save money on marketing management fees

- discover your USP and enjoy dentistry

- improve accountability within your business

- work out where you are losing money and new patients

- improve reception skills.

Who is Grant McAree?

Grant McAree:

- is a passionate dental mentor, through and through. Wears his heart on his sleeve and has gained a reputation as the 'no nonsense, tell all' dentist on social media. His *Ugly Truth* videos have now been watched hundreds of thousands of times across the globe, earning him a Marmite reputation. You either love him or you don't but listen to what he has to say – he has seen it and worn the T-shirt and is happy to tell all

- won the award for the most patients treated globally by IAS Academy in 2018. Whilst his gross would be considered very high for a 3-day week, his mantra is 'do the right treatment on the right patient at the right time with the right support'.

He has:

- created a Facebook page with over 6.5 thousand dentists and marketers

- built six dental squat practices

- sold 5 million pounds' worth of dental businesses

- achieved only two O levels yet managed to get two degrees and become a dentist

- built one of the fastest growing dental chatbots and CRM systems

- mentored dentists worldwide

- launched sell-out courses for dentists to learn about dental marketing and business

- been the runner-up for a dental industry award for his marketing and advertising course

- become a Diamond Invisalign provider

- built the fastest growing and one of the largest private squat practices in Devon over a four-year period

- voted for but failed to make the top 50 most influential dentists in the UK. Maybe next year!

Connect with Grant:
- www.dentalbusinessmentor.co.uk
- https://www.facebook.com/groups/511575225902292
- https://www.facebook.com/DrGrantMcAreeBDS/
- https://www.instagram.com/dentalbusinessmentor/
- Email : grantmcaree@gmail.com
- Tel : 07896877827

How to use this book

You may be sitting there thinking this is just another book; you will have a read and then forget about it all. But I will show you exercises and videos, and I will give you free tips and tricks that you can use the very next day. But the massive take-home message? You are normal, what you are going through and the stresses you may or may not be experiencing are all normal. The ups and downs of dentistry and the running of a business come with sacrifices. This book will show you how to ensure those sacrifices do not cost you any more than they need to. You will be able to take back control and fill the holes in your business bucket. The holes that are draining your business.

I just want you to consider there is an alternative way to run a business. We all get into the habit of doing the job. It is so hard to break that cycle when we do dentistry. I just want you to consider there is an alternative! An easier way! A more productive approach to the business of dentistry.

I would like to thank you for starting this journey. It takes great courage to change. Change makes many of us feel fear. The fear can be so overwhelming that change never happens. So, you have gone this far, and I would like to personally welcome you to that change. Which is going to start now.

I promise you this. If you read this book – if you carry out the exercises and go one step further and read the resources – you will discover that this is not just another boring book with crap pictures and useless tips that are irrelevant and unhelpful. It isn't a book that has the pages filled out with photographs and snazzy but useless graphics. It is a tell-all book full of practical, transformative information and techniques that have been tried and tested.

_____

You are normal, what you are going through and the stresses you may or may not be experiencing are all normal.

_____

The information provided is what will drive you towards a more effectively run business, and it can save you millions over a career. Take action; do the exercises. Don't just read the book, but make it come alive. Turn words into action and you will see that all this stuff, all this business of dentistry, 'it ain't rocket science.'

I have put together a Resource Pack (including tasks), which not only enhances your experience of the book but it will give you vital information that will help you on your journey, making your progress much quicker and easier. There is everything from consultation templates to full clinical notes. Also included are videos that give you step-by-step instructions on how to set up a free CRM, how to design a paid advert, how to target dentists for associate positions, how to SEO and write a blog, and how to set up Facebook and Instagram saved responses (this will save you hours of time responding to useless questions about teeth whitening and the cost of a filling). I also give away free reception templates that will enable you to provide that customer care everyone dreams about! In short, this is not just your average book! The pack will help make life easier for you and improve the care you are providing your patients, safely and ethically. So, to summarise, it will save you money!

Included in the Resource Pack:

Tasks
1. Create a social media advert using my easy-to-follow design.

2. Download the Strategy Tree For Dentists PDF and structure your business more effectively.

3. A contract review, a 1-2-1 HR consultation and a compliance health check with Phil Clark from Peninsula.

4. How to SEO a dental blog on a WordPress website.

5. Mystery shop form. Put your reception staff to the test.

6. Download a free CRM template (customer relationship manager) www.trello.com.

7. Download the 360 degrees feedback form.

8. Download the Instagram treatment saved replies for patients.

9. Download template email replies to patients.

10. A list of the five questions reception can use to build rapport.

11. Watch a video demonstrating how to create your own CRM.

12. Download my consultation notes for Invisalign to help you stay out of trouble.

13. Download the hourly clinic rate spreadsheet.

Head over to **www.dentalbusinessmentor.co.uk/resourcepack** (password: rocketscience) to gain access to the resource area of my website where all these tools are waiting for you.

I want to say a massive congratulations. You are about to learn a very different approach to dentistry and how to build, develop and run a dental business. Some of the stories you will be able to relate to. Other stories may be a bit close to the bone (I don't hold back). For now, go on over to the Resource Pack and download all the free 'stuff' I have learnt, accumulated and utilised when building some of the largest squat practices in my area – and on a shoestring budget too.

Why did I write this book?

I chose a job where the feeling of isolation is common – it doesn't have to be that way. I have grown into a different person now. It's called maturity! I found myself wanting to bond, meet others and share my experiences. I spent an entire lifetime building my businesses behind closed doors – almost in secret. Now I want to bust these secrets open and share everything!

When I started sharing – my passion grew. I now feel I want to share my ups and downs and, in doing so, help others. Sharing is now part of my USP. Sharing for me is everything. This is what inspired me to start a Facebook group, organise courses and, now, write this book.

I used to be the dentist that ran out of the BDA meetings unable to talk to anyone. It is a more natural and easy way to live. In writing this book it really has made me realise just how isolated we, as dentists can become. In the words of Jerry Maguire – it was just a mission statement. Then the flood gates opened!

CHAPTER 1

THE UGLY TRUTH

Suicide in dentistry – the unwanted link 05/10/2020:
The British Dental Journal stated that 17.6% of dentists
surveyed admitted to having seriously considered suicide.

I do know this – dentistry online – is not real-life dentistry. It isn't just about fast cars, beautiful houses, perfect lives and loads of money. There is always a sacrifice behind every successful smile you see. There is always a price to pay. It just depends on what price you are willing to pay for that success. Meet William. I've met hundreds of Williams in my time, in fact part of me used to be a bit like him. Let me show you how hard a day in the life of William really is right now...

Fear starts way before William wakes up. It starts the minute his head hits the pillow at night. That daunting feeling of drifting into a sleep you just hope and pray will be a restful one. A deep one when you can just forget the rubbish that will be unleashed the minute you walk through your dental practice front door. William drifts into no man's land. Before sleep, yet not awake. The worries from the day invade his mind – he gets that electrifying awakeness. Glancing over to the clock. Heck – he has only been asleep for 35 minutes. Now there are eight hours to think about his day list tomorrow. He shouldn't have looked at it before leaving work the day before. Mrs Smith first thing. A crown fit. William thinks she hates him – he may be right. He realises now he shouldn't have started the treatment (that red flag feeling we sometimes choose to ignore) and she now wants to punish him. The crown will have to be nothing less than perfect for Mrs Smith. He is not good enough to make that perfect crown. He thinks back to a course he once attended. He can't even remember the technique to make the crown perfect. All charged up after that course. Shame he hadn't put the skills he had learnt to better use. This is the fourth retry! He feels as bad as the rubbish crown being fitted tomorrow at 7.30am. Yes, 7.30am. Normal start time is 9. How did that happen? Great, he now worries he is going to annoy the entire staff asking them to come in early. Let's add to the list of reasons for feeling crap.

William just feels so negative today. He just needs sleep. Best he doesn't wake the wife. He slips down the stairs and has a little relaxer. A small swig of whiskey. That will help. There seems to be a massive struggle just to feel happy right now. As he sits in the kitchen he looks out at the massive garden. Yep – tick. He will photograph that tomorrow morning – the entire profession will see and admire his success. But they will probably miss out the fat pillock that is reflecting back at him in the window – that won't look good in any photo! Yep – leave that one out. He had been planning to lose weight. What happened? He used to be thin and handsome. Fat, forty and fired. Great book. He feels like that – at least he can't be fired. Unless of course Mrs Smith contacts the General Dental Council. It could all be taken away in the blink of an eye.

The morning light is unwelcome. Especially after an anxious fitful sleep. The good old days when no one cared – student life seems a long time ago. However, today will be a good day. William tries to think positively. He is suddenly starving. Oh, sod the diet – he needs the strength to survive Mrs Smith. Diet starts tonight. He pulls his clothes off the Peloton Bike. The bike he bought to lose weight. It is a flipping glorified clothes horse. A £2k clothes horse. Could be a perfect social media post if he sat on it pretending to exercise. Maybe a photograph of his knee. With a backdrop of the garden. Heck, if he drives his Porsche round into the garden and makes the kids play outside – same time – he will look fantastic. Yes, that's another tick and another post that confirms his total success in the dental world. Happiness seems to be inversely proportional to these bragging posts. The unhappier William becomes, the greater his need to post his house, cars and apparent wealth and apparently perfect life.

Let me tell you, it is far from perfect. He yearns for quiet and no stress, and he just wants to feel normal again. If only for a short while.

The drive to work is where William finds a safe place to relax. He eats a bit more, spills coffee whilst changing the gears, drops crumbs everywhere. His diet is so badly managed. He hardly eats – yet seems to put on weight. Starving himself in the day and eating like a horse at night. What happened to three balanced meals!? Squeezing out of his low, cramped car, the belly prevents an easy exit. Easy exit! That's a term for it – he falls out onto the pavement. This will be the last laugh of the day. He is about to enter hell. Key in hand. The feeling of the car ride is a distant memory. Here we go: turn the key – Armageddon.

William walks into the reception area. He knows the dragon behind the desk is equally as bad as the GP receptionists up the road but, frankly, she scares him. If he listened to her talk on the phone, he would do his usual – retreat into the surgery. Out of sight, out of mind. He decides he will address that like his weight issue. Another day. Mrs Dragon pants as she informs William Mrs Smith phoned up yesterday and cancelled. What the hell? Could you not have told me yesterday? He so wanted to end that treatment. Another night, another anxious evening. When has she rebooked? 'Oh, don't worry,' Dragon returns reassuringly, 'She didn't rebook – just wants her notes and all radiographs.' He just wanted to call Dragon lady a total dick, but employment law prevents such an outburst. Employment law! That's a joke. He knows nothing about that. His staff run the joint. Anyway, now he has dental solicitors, GDC and the rubbish crown he plans to squeeze on to top off his perfect day.

William will go over Mrs Smith's notes 100 times until he finds an error to obsess about. He will then print out the notes, take them home – yes, they will occupy him, probably all evening. He will box that worry. He can phone his indemnity, but they will probably say they won't support him. Maybe he should try to resolve the issue before phoning them. Yes, if and when the letter arrives, he will attempt to take the beginning bit on himself so the indemnity company won't increase his monthly subs. Coupled with the fact that they are assisting him with another issue, it means they will see him as a total train wreck and dump him on the spot. He feels so alone. Hey, it's 8am – his day starts. He fires up that bad boy computer and sees what his day looks like. Staring blankly at the appointment book. Oh, dear lord. Do all his patients who hate him ring each other and decide to book on the same day, seriously?

Would you believe it if William said he forgot to go to the toilet one day? Near on wet himself on one occasion. He simply forgot to look after his body. Bent over double for eight hours a day. The sweat dripped down his back entering the crack of his ass. I never knew this was possible: sweat dripping down your entire body!

Every patient reminds William of the hell that awaits him with Mrs Smith. He treats every patient with an element of paranoia. There is that image embedded in his psyche – they are all planning to take him to court. Treatment plans become safe and totally risk free. He risks losing a fortune by being super safe, by being afraid to step out of his totally safe and secure zone. He awaits that letter from the lawyers with morbid anticipation. He awaits the end of his career. The garden and the Porsche will be gone forever. The life he has worked so hard to obtain will be flushed down the toilet. He didn't think his life would turn out like this. He felt so positive when he started out. How did it get so tough? How did William get here? When he started out it was the golden years of dentistry.

He manages to see the day through (survive!) on adrenaline. No lunch. That is the diet plan. Loads of coffee. Putting out fires everywhere. The end of the day arrives. A welcome bell goes off in his head. Home time. He will read Mrs Smith's notes at tea. Ignore his wife again. Children are growing up so fast. As he looks in the mirror in his supercar, William wonders what awaits him at home. What is he thinking about? Is he in Groundhog Day? Different day, same problems.

The day finally ends after the last appointment. What a joke. He is always late. Always late home. He knows the staff have been moaning all day, sending messages on SOE. He treats it as background noise. Garbage. He has zero time for their moaning or their feedback. He knows he should listen but, to be honest, he just hasn't the strength to put on a lovely smile when all he wants to do is punch them in the face for being so ungrateful.

His family don't understand the pressure. The reason he does all this is for them. Deep down he knows that's horseshit. He does it for himself. To heal the wounds he has carried for years. How does he know that? His wife always says she would prefer less money and more time with him. So, it must be down to him. He is so bloody tired.

The kids talk to William. He hears them. He is not sure he is actually listening. Sod it, they won't be able to tell, he convinces himself. They talk to him about some stuff going on in their lives, but Mrs Smith is a big-boy problem. William's thoughts spiral out of control. He can't relax.

A drink. He knows it's wrong but it takes the stress away. He needs to get better and get control. Maybe tomorrow. What a difference a day can make. He watches the clock. Soon to bed. His back hurts, his brain has this fog. The fog – this is what he sometimes calls peace. In reality, he is just smashed and can't spare another thought. William looks at the clock again. His wife talks about the programme they have been watching for two hours. Hell, he lost time – he always loses time. Bed soon. Groundhog Day. Let's Finnegan Begin Again.

He often thinks about slowing down. But it's the money. The commitments. The fast cars and private school fees. The social media pressure. Every other bugger makes it look like a piece of cake. He will be a laughing stock. How can he slow down? Like a wheel hurtling down the hill. In truth, he doesn't know how to slow down. How to ease off the gas. He knows it's the right thing to do, but failure is not an option. Not in this dojo. 'Oh get lost, Karate Kid. You suck', William mutters to himself. He knows he will hit a wall, but William has got a lot more in him. He is resilient. Just one more year. What a difference a year can make!

If you can relate to William's story you are not alone. I don't necessarily mean all of his troubles and experiences. Maybe just some of them. The sad fact is some dentists experience all the above and more. I meet dentists every week who are dealing with some of William's issues. When you are at that point in your life, realising you need to slow down, you have already passed the point of an easy return. Coming back from mental exhaustion can be a slow and painful road to recovery.

Most dentists are brilliantly clever – high IQs – yet struggle to run a business and juggle family life. I see it up and down the country. But consider this: lawyers, dentists, medics, accountants, pharmacists – they were never taught business at university. My former accountant was a typical example. A terrible businessman. But when we work in an industry reliant on business, and we were never taught that business, stress soon follows. This is then coupled with the way we are remunerated. 'I need to make sure I get more patients than that competitor up the road, who I seem to always end up talking to at BDA meetings.' Until it changes it will continue to be a struggle. A struggle to learn business, a struggle to reach out for support, a struggle to know where to turn.

In my experience, dental partnerships start out positively – I don't think I have ever met the Ant and Dec of dentistry. It always seems to end with one or both thinking the other is a complete dick. If you have survived the business partner minefield you are a better person than I. Partnerships are something I have tried to avoid during my career. My dad (a retired dentist) suffered over and over again as a result of the dentists he chose to be partners with. In those days it was the golden years, and dentists made a lot of money. But the back-stabbing and ruthlessness of partnerships saw many dentists drop out and leave the profession.

As Jerry Maguire so finely put it: 'we live in a world of tough competitorship', and we do. Dog eat dog. In my experience, with all the countless dentists I have met, I can assure you of one thing: if you are struggling – you are not alone. If you have grey hair on your balls (or equivalent), meaning you are of a particular age, it means that the golden years of dentistry have passed and life will never be as it was when you first qualified. We live in a time where over-regulation is commonplace, notes have to be masterpieces, staff are in charge and a chronic lack of nurses and hygienists will make running a business extremely challenging. To survive you will have to be the best you can be. And then better than that!

I have run many courses on building dental businesses, creating knockout open days, supporting colleagues in distress, locating and developing squat practices, discovering USPs. I have mentored and coached hundreds of dentists. I don't care to debate the difference between a coach and a mentor.

I have helped, guided, and supported dentists from all walks of life. I have found that we have picked a profession with the highest rate of divorce, alcoholism and depression. A recent BDJ study showed that over half of dentists say stress in their job exceeded their ability to cope. They say that a stressful job is when the individual experiences five to seven stress triggers per day. Five to seven! I remember the days I experienced that per hour! Per patient!

We are good people. We go to work to do better, but we hear 'I hate you – I hate the dentist' up to 30 times a day. What other job has to endure this response from their clients? It grinds you down. All those irritating comments patients come out with: 'What made you do this awful job?', 'He won't hurt you, little Johnny', 'I hate you', 'I hate needles' and 'dentistry is so expensive.' Yes, dentistry is expensive, but so are their £1,000 phone and packet of fags they drop as they jump into your chair, ripping the leather with a pen they left in their pocket. With their teeth falling out, abscesses, decay and appalling oral hygiene, they ask to make their front tooth look a little better for a wedding in two weeks. All for the asking price of a UDA!

Who would want to be a dentist? Is it possible to survive without burning out at least once in a dental career? (I have been at my lowest approximately three times in 25 years!) Many of the dentists I have met are all in different stages of burnout. I would say as many as 50% range from feeling dog-tired to being completely exhausted. I can safely say I don't think I have met a totally secure, happy, contented dentist with the perfect life. I am sure there are many dentists reading this and disagreeing. Lean over and ask your partner. Or are you alone? I think everyone is searching for the answer that will give them true happiness and total fulfilment. I am not saying dentistry is a miserable job, but it is a bloody hard slog at times.

Research by the BDA shows that dentistry is associated with high levels of stress and burnout, with 17.6% of dentists surveyed admitting to having seriously considered committing suicide and, between 1995 and 2011, 77 dentists died as a result of taking their own lives. How bad is that? This is a fact. Google it. But let's not be too negative. Let's just consider the more minor psychological ailments – unhappiness, stress, intrusive thoughts, sexual dysfunction, divorce, alcoholism, sadness, anxiety. There are many emotions that come before suicidal ideation. What I am trying to say is that what you are experiencing is the norm in our job. How bloody sad is that!? What I hope you take from my book is that it is normal, there is a way out, there is a way to separate the wood from the trees. You just have to have a little bit of knowledge on how to get there and a load of courage. However, until you have the knowledge, no amount of courage will steer you in the right direction. Dolly Parton (love her) said, 'You cannot change the wind, but you can adjust the sails.' You just need to make the change and know the change is not the wrong one! And then, my friends, 'it is plain sailing.'

The tragedy about all of this is that it isn't anyone's fault when we find ourselves in these sometimes unbearable situations. I am not gonna lie: depression and anxiety are absolutely vile. They suck the life and soul out of the best of us. However, if there is a small bit of advice I can offer from my experience, it's this: you are certainly not alone if you do suffer from stress. And it certainly isn't your fault. The odds are stacked against us. I suppose we could break it down. Yep, it is safe to say that the day you step on that podium to accept your degree – I got a slipper across the head (Dundee Graduates will recognise this tradition) – you are entering a world that will either make or break you. We are thrown into the lion's den without a spear. Everyone in the dental world I know who has been there for a number of years has had a time on the edge. So, why do I think this stress is so very real in the world of drilling teeth? Sometimes, I hear myself saying, 'They're only teeth', but we all know it is so very much more than that.

Are we taught business at university? I can't remember one class or workshop. Not even a hands-on discussion in between clinic and lunch. Why couldn't they have got a local businessman in to teach us the basics? Whet our appetite. Surely that is what teaching is about. Planting the seed and letting the student nurture that information. Growing the passion. If we had known the struggles back then, many of us would have diverted our interests, changed our plans. So, if you have no clue about how to run a business, you have to learn on the job. A very stressful and expensive exercise. What is the saying for this approach? 'Learn from your mistakes'? People say this is the best way to educate yourself. Complete bollocks. I disagree totally. We need a grounding to make simple decisions. They wouldn't teach a surgeon to transplant a heart by throwing them in at the deep end! Well, welcome to the business of dentistry. 'Here are the keys to your new place, Doc. Here are a couple of members of staff who will cause you endless headaches, and make sure you get marketing for more patients because if you don't bring in the money, we will take the building back and your family home as well.' The new dental entrepreneur will be eating and sleeping the business with an internal fear of failure and a lack of support in a highly regulated environment. It will be like flipping a coin. Red or black. Will they survive and manage to cut the mustard, or will they end up stressed and burnt-out, regretting their decision for a decade or two?

Knowing where to get educated, that is the key. I have heard that banks help dentists, but that is when they are almost at the point of failure. Teams are sent in to see if they can rescue the sinking ship. Who would know the ins and outs of learning about the business of dentistry? Many of us are reluctant to reach out to successful colleagues. There is a real fear of being ridiculed. So, for now, most dentists learn from their mistakes. Many live day by day, putting out the fires, making knee-jerk reactions and decisions.

The staff will then recognise the owner's weaknesses. They ask for future pay rises, and the dentists then make promises they won't keep, making snap decisions and poorly thought-out plans. When you are working too much in the business, as opposed to on it, you can't seem to be able to reflect. Reflection is the one thing that is vital when running a business. An opportunity to sit back and look from the outside. It gives you a sense of calm. A place where decisions can be made and plans can be developed.

Many dentists are stuck with how busy they are. They are said to be a victim of their own success. Starting at 7.30am and working through until 7.30pm, seven days a week. Back in the day, I chose to work hours like this, as I thought that the more time I spent seeing patients the more money came in, and the more I would earn. This would mean fewer problems and it would reduce the financial burden of running the business. What I didn't see was the impact it had on my health. I couldn't seem to step back and reflect and make the right decisions. I didn't realise that a dentist doing four days a week could gross as much as a dentist doing six days. How could that be? I was a creature of habit. I kept up those long hours for many years. I didn't see that the hours I put in hindered not only my health but my overall success. I didn't see it at all; I was blind.

So, without direction and without a moment to breathe, how can you plan? How can you make a decent strategy? As human beings, I think it is within us all to do better. To develop. It's a part of nature, a kind of evolution. We see it everywhere: jaws are getting smaller, appendixes are no longer essential, due to diet changes. It's the same in business; we want to be a better businessman tomorrow, but with all this stacked up against us – internal and external factors – how can we possibly succeed and prosper? I have seen, on many occasions, dentists getting their wallet out to pay for an advert only to then put it away due to the worry about making another stupid decision. The lack of knowledge and fear of failure is what kills most dental businesses before they can progress. Alongside, of course, being dog-tired without a moment to reflect.

The majority of dentists are extremely academic, bright and very caring members of our community. We just have everything stacked up against us when it comes to the business of dentistry. We work in a small area of the body. Our focus can be on something 1cm squared for three hours at a time. We barely have time to go to the toilet. The majority of our patients would prefer to be someplace else. Oh, and we have to ask our clients to pay for the privilege of being somewhere

---

The lack of knowledge and fear of failure is what kills most dental businesses before they can progress.

---

they would prefer not to be. There aren't many jobs that have the odds so stacked against them. No time to look up and take a deep breath, have a meal, take a dump, say hello to our partners. 'When on earth do I have time to run a dental business with all those odds stacked up against me?', a dentist I know used to joke. He worked so hard, when he got home his kids asked their mum who this strange bloke was in the house. A joke maybe, but the truth is not a million miles off that. The ugly truth is that dentistry is tough, and we just need to learn to breathe and to step back. To work on the business and not just in it.

Someone said to me once, 'You aren't living, Grant. You are merely surviving.' Oh, get stuffed. What did they know? I owned a ten-surgery practice. I was alive. I was somebody. People knew me. But I suppose I was just increasing the bucket size and pouring more water into it when the thing had holes everywhere; I wasn't solving the problem. It might work for a while. For example, you can hire a marketing agency only to throw more leads at a broken system. The marketer then gets the blame for rubbish leads. It doesn't matter if the dragon receptionist is rude – but we all like to divert blame.

Yes, I blamed the marketer. I just want a marketer to sit down and talk to me. To explain a strategy. Yes, that was the problem. Wait a minute. When did I have time to do that? Surely, I paid them to take that part of the business away from me. So, I can safely say to anyone reading this book: stop throwing more water into a broken bucket. It ain't rocket science. Still, I was there for years, until one day it hit me; it was a lightbulb moment. Nothing in business is in isolation. It is a chain. Any part of that chain can be broken, and if it is, it all fails. But you can mend the breaks. Small improvements across the board are far better than large improvements in one area.

So, helping dental businesses improve is about understanding all the key elements of a practice. Where they are bleeding, losing patients, it isn't about marketing hacks. Oh, come on – of course it is about marketing hacks. Free tips and tricks. We dentists, we all love a freebie. We are all bloody sick and tired of that dental tax, the extra fees companies put on our bill as they think we are loaded. We want a quick fix, like drilling that tooth – get in, drill and get out – and that is fine, you know. It is OK to do some flashy marketing hacks. I have my top 10 free hacks (also in the Resource Pack...) but – and it is a massive but – the business needs to function as a whole, not in parts. Would you believe me if I said I carried out 132 mystery shops last year? 130 failed miserably. That is staggering; no number of new patients will mend that. The saddest part of the story was that my surgery was one of the 130! Point being – train your staff, get good systems in place and constantly monitor the wheels that turn your business.

I have seen dentists go from zero to hero within as little as a month. I don't mean making more dosh. I always tell my children that, if you enjoy what you do and are good at it, the money will be there. You just have to be patient. My hero is the dentist who makes life changes by reducing alcohol intake, losing weight, getting fit, spending more time with their loved ones, experiencing less stress, and being happier and more in control. They start to work on the business and manage to catch a thought; knee jerk reactions are no longer a business strategy. They are living life and no longer just surviving. We are dead for a long time. I have worked with many dentists from many walks of life: all ages, all with different goals, all motivated by different things. There is one truth: dentists are good people. They all mean well and want to do a good job. The tragedy is that some can get a little lost along the way; some may slag off a colleague, take drugs, or drink too much, but they never set out to be this way.

However, it isn't all doom and gloom. Many dentists I have worked with have turned their lives around, built their dream squat, and felt more in control. Fear was holding them back; most of that fear was created by social media posts claiming they would be broke for the first three years if they started a new business. Watching someone take control of their life is exhilarating.

When you get to the crossroads towards the end of a career – I am at those crossroads – you either keep all that experience you have gained locked away, keep it hidden, or you share it. In sharing it, the knowledge grows and you encourage others to share it too, becoming part of the evolutionary process of development. That is something I love, my passion, and my goal for the latter part of my career: make a difference. Make someone's life better and more tolerable. That is what brings me joy now. Not everyone will experience the stress I have experienced. I do think it is down to personality types. Some people can remain detached and, on occasions, unaware of their feelings. I have met some very happy and content dentists. They seem to be able to take life less seriously than I, managing to cope with the stresses that dentistry throws at them. I am left with a tinge of jealousy when I encounter these people. Is it possible to be a well-rounded, content, happy dentist? Only you can answer that question, but for me, this is my story.

CHAPTER 2

MY STORY

I wish I could find a reason for the suffering I went through. I can safely say I have been to hell and back with my emotions and insecurities, but my life has been pretty normal. I had some challenges for sure. I have two loving parents and I was educated privately. I do remember I wanted to be the best; I didn't give a toss about personal achievements – I just wanted to be the best.

Do you know there are only five passions in life? We have a mixture of all five, although some are more dominant. To feel, to acquire, to defend, to learn and to bond. My top two are to acquire and to defend. If anyone tries to take what is mine, watch out because I am coming for you. To learn is probably last in the line-up. I wouldn't have thought that – I have two degrees. However, I remember leaving dental school thinking I would never take another exam. In fact, I came to the conclusion that all the studying resulted in my first nervous breakdown. Maybe not a breakdown as I look back. Just a moment in my life where everything just didn't seem to add up or make sense. Safe to say, I was emotionally stunted. But I had two degrees. I remember thinking that this hollow feeling I carried like a dead dog in a bag would be released if I made a load of dosh, had a big house, loads of staff, a sportscar, motorboat and loads of property. My aim was to buy and build a shed load of dental businesses. I felt powerful as staff listened to me and respected me. I didn't realise at the time that people only pretend to listen to their employers. In the words of Julia Roberts: 'Only because you are paying me to.' My employees didn't necessarily respect me; it was just because I signed the cheque at the end of the month.

However, saddled with all my emotional crap, I embarked on a career that had a high level of suicide, alcohol addiction and divorce. Still, you know what? I felt I was invincible. Well, that is a distorted way to think and the recipe for the disaster that occurred a little later down the road. Still, hey, tomorrow is tomorrow, so who gives a damn? I was living for the moment, not realising the damage I was doing to myself.

I scraped a pass at dental school and off I went in my clapped-out Mini Metro down to Penzance. I remember waving my parents goodbye, shouting back, 'I am off to make my millions.' I won't go into the details of why I chose Cornwall – chasing childhood memories, I suppose. However, people grow up and move on – the place I grew up in had changed. I remember arriving on day one. It was a depressed town, filled with homelessness, shops boarded up. (I should have realised the area was not that great when they offered post grads £1,000 just to move there!) Day two, I couldn't wait to get away and then get on with my life: get a business of my own, get a life and finally be happy. You see, I always wanted the next thing. The next thing would make me happy. I just had this drive to change, to adapt, to modify. It was a pattern that probably made me successful and wealthy! A pattern that possibly led to a lot of loneliness, poor choices and instability.

Twelve months out of college, I marched into the bank, debt up to my eyeballs, and set about my plan to take over the world. Plan? It was not really a plan, merely a statement. I bought a massive house on the main street of Plympton (a small town on the outskirts of Plymouth) and started filling it with dentists.

I had finally arrived. I had made my mark on the world, been the new kid on the block. I could afford to buy sports cars and houses, eating in fancy restaurants. I bought a jet boat called 'The Wet Beaver'. Needless to say, I must have looked like a complete pillock. However, to me, I was living the dream. Although, looking back, I was incredibly lonely, it was a loneliness that would serve me well as a dental business owner, a feeling I would become accustomed to. Life can be a real bitch, but now I realise that all our experiences serve us well in the end. A lot of my darker experiences in life helped me be the salesman I am today. My mother always said I could sell anything to anybody. 'Talking my way out of a paper bag' she called it. I am good at that, and I have passed that skill on to my children. A gift, as I see it. We sell every day. I know the art of selling is frowned upon in dentistry. In reality, we are always selling: I sell to the kids the idea that they should go and do their homework, or go to bed at night, and I use it to get lucky with my wife. I have always said foreplay starts when you get out of bed in the morning, not when you jump in at night, so my success in my marriage is through selling every day, all day. And I never stop. I am just blessed that I have such a loving wife, as without her I don't think I would have survived this mad crazy thing they call life.

So, when did I realise I had to make a change? When did I have that lightbulb moment? That turn in the road. Truth is there was no lightbulb moment. I hit rock bottom. That is, after all, the most suitable place to turn around and start swimming back up. I was a young millionaire, lonely, incapable of holding down a relationship, unaware and without respect for other people's emotional boundaries. I had no clue about life and love. It's as though I missed all that rubbish when they taught it at school. So, you could probably define me as 'the functional millionaire depressive'.

A day in the life of the functional millionaire depressive. I felt alive at work. It was all I had. It made me feel worthy of all the education and costs that went into creating the masterpiece that stared back at me in the mirror. Oh, I had people who wanted to spend time with me. When you are lost, you attract lost souls; it's sort of like two people make a complete person. Back to Jerry Maguire saying, 'you complete me' … what a pile of rubbish. You need to complete yourself to feel happy and content with someone else. I felt my staff completed me, my business and the fortune I was building. So, when it didn't go just like I had planned, when a staff member ignored me, when someone handed in their notice, when patients complained, when I was asked for a pay rise from an ungrateful plonker, I never realised why my world felt like it had collapsed in. Reflecting back, I looked for external validation everywhere and in everything I did.

So, what were the issues I experienced at work? They were issues I am sure you can relate to. It was usually staff. Oh, I see staff photos posted on social media: they all look happy and content, although mine always seemed annoyed. I remember at one point my staff became so demanding that it almost broke my manager. I always diverted staff to the management team, avoiding the constant complaining about pay or the demanding hours. Staff would phone in sick, and I wanted to shout down the phone. I always wondered why they didn't have the same work ethic as I did. It never bloody dawned on me it was because they were paid £6 an hour and I drove to work in a fast flashy car.

Staff were fighting with each other. Dentists were demanding and shouting at their nurses. Dentists thought they ran the business yet did not accept any responsibility for driving the business forward. Dental associates – I was one once – were probably the most demanding and irritating of the lot. But bloody hell, when you become a principal you witness this first hand. A badly run business will see the associates go home with a larger income than the owner! They would swan in demanding a reason for a gap in their appointment book, or a specific nurse not being available, or they wanted the most expensive equipment and materials. Please, run your own business and you will see the other side. You will see that there isn't an abundance of cash. It can be a nightmare steering the ship and there are sacrifices to be made, both financially and personally.

I just had a dire need for external validation. I bent over backwards to please everyone, even the ungrateful associates, but the lack of love in my life, the loneliness that accompanied work and growth, the need to be noticed, it all led me to a stranger's door. A little Irish lady who made up for her stature with confidence and kindness. I remember my opening words to her, 'I am totally bloody miserable and have no right to be as I am rich and successful.' From that point onwards a light slowly came on. I slowly but surely became the person I should have been all along.

So, how did therapy help me with my dental business? Would I recommend therapy to everyone? Bloody right I would. Why?

The journey to self-discovery can be a painful one, but the outcome and benefits are staggering. So, how did it all change my approach? How did my business benefit from the utterly heart-wrenching journey my therapist, Grace Chatting, took me on? I look at my therapist and a saying keeps popping into my head, although I can't even remember where I heard it: 'whoever saves one life saves the world entire'. I have passed on skills I learnt during therapy to my children, so if you ever want to consider therapy, it can save entire generations. But back to the business of dentistry...

I was putting out fires, snappy and oversensitive. Oh, how badly did I deal with situations! However, there were situations I would still struggle to deal with today, even with all of my experience, like the nurse complaining about being asked to clean up menstrual blood from a dentist's chair, but across the board I was probably quite threatening in nature. I was defensive and unapproachable. I had zero tolerance and was wounded quite easily and regularly. It just seemed to always be a battle. A day at the surgery was like going to war every bloody day! I can say that the turnaround was an emotional lightbulb going on moment for me. As I got my head organised, I started to look at the business in a different light. I gave myself the time to look around and strategically plan rather than running from fire to fire.

How did I turn it all around?

1. I learned to manage my own emotions

As soon as I recognised my own emotional boundaries and respected others, my stress levels reduced significantly. I was not there to rescue other people, and I was not there to be rescued. I removed myself from being the villain, and I chose to step back from the regular dramas that occur with staff and associates: the Karpman drama triangle (look that one up, it's a life-changer) suggests that you can reach out and not attempt to save the other person. You can be honest and not use honesty as a blunt weapon; you can ask for help without expecting to be rescued. My business started to feel less like a constant drama. It started to become a more functional tool. The staff turnover slowed down. People stopped gossiping about one another. When you are at the top, the staff look to you for direction. If you have poor personal boundaries, this will be fed down the chain. It will spread out like a virus.

2. I got better at dealing with confrontation

Oh, I wish I was 18 again. I would use this as a life lesson, never mind in the dental practice. Grace called it DESC. This will be described in depth in the 'People' chapter. If someone or something really ticks you off, you need a response that is balanced, fair and enables a suitable outcome. I will share this secret with you all now. I will give you an example of how it worked in my world, in the world we call the business of dentistry.

We all have experienced reception staff that are difficult to manage. Any feedback, whether constructive or otherwise, ends in a moodiness and an apathy towards hard work for a few days. On occasions it can go into weeks of sad faces and bad attitudes. Worse still, they seem so highly strung you are worried about saying anything, as they will hand their notice in, leaving you deep in the mire. You are faced with that decision, and it is tough. I remember it. Should you approach the receptionist or should you just let it slide for another six months? Or you could try the DESC technique! It is a ninja move! Done properly, it is impossible to lose the confrontation! On a side note, this technique works in all other areas of life, not just dentistry!

As soon as you begin to become triumphant with confrontations you go to your quiet place alone (mine was on the bog as I could kill two birds with one stone – think and park fudge), pat yourself on the back at the win, then phone your HR company to get back-up and further advice. Meanwhile, the dragon is outside drumming up support with other members of staff who are equally ungrateful.

Confrontations in the dental practice are common. When you start to lose control of staff it is a tough climb back. It is so bloody lonely out there in the wilderness on your own. Hence why a lot of dentists bring in their husbands and wives, who help screw everything up in double-quick time. However, to gain control doesn't mean to control. It means your feelings do not dominate your decisions. You are not left with a 'I wish I could have said that' or a 'I wish I had said that'; basically, your interpersonal skills will improve with confidence.

When you describe the effect it had on you – it makes you actually feel your feelings – I call it 'lighting up the darkness'. When you feel the energy of the emotion you have, it subsides and loses its hold on you. You allow the chemical reaction. You make better decisions. You will no longer make decisions based on a mixture of bad feelings. Feel the fear and do it anyway. Yes, jump out a plane and shout damn and hell, but at work you just need to have an element of confidence and self-control to survive the day.

When you become a better leader, everything functions more smoothly, the business seems to fall in line with your actions and directions. Confidence is always a winner. No one can take that away. You have clarity of mind and the entire culture of the business changes. You feel energised. You make better decisions, like dropping your hours and working on the business and not in it, and guess what? Yep, profit goes up. It just works. So, from the feeling of being resigned to eventual burnout, I became energised. I felt I was winning.

I can say that, with all my therapy and the experiences I have gone through in business, I do feel wiser. When I see colleagues struggling, it does fill me with sadness. I also get frustrated at a lot of advice that is given to young dentists that I feel is quite damaging to the profession. For example, labelling leads as 'bad' or 'poor'. We mustn't forget that leads are human beings. My teenage daughter, Mia McAree, advised me over dinner one evening, that it feels good to do something nice. For that reason alone we should treat all patients nicely, no matter if they are shopping around and not ready to buy.

We should treat all patients nicely, no matter if they are shopping around and not ready to buy.

Dentistry isn't all this social media nonsense: fast cars, money, perfect lives and perfect treatment outcomes. I know it is a step too far, but no one will ever post their rubbish cases, their stressed lives, their failed marriages – still, at least it would show some balance. I truly believe social media does the dental profession no favours, and it is quite false.

When I came through the difficult times, I called them 'emotional lightbulb moments'. Those are the points when you suddenly realise what's been holding you back. You drop the dead dog, loosen the chains. Stress falls away, firm friendships can be made, falling in love is possible, businesses can be built and developed, staff are more appreciative (not all – I won't get too carried away – a lot are still plain assholes who need major amounts of therapy).

To share my experiences is now my goal, showing people that even though you can be on your knees with stress, depression and anxiety, anything is still possible. I remember when times were tough that I had a tea towel. Between patients, I used to go and wring it out violently in the toilet. I was trying to balance my physical state with my mental one. I just wanted balance. I have achieved that now. The final piece to my puzzle is sharing these experiences, whether it is my Dental Business & Marketing course or my Facebook group. Whether it is a phone call or my Squat Build course, it is all about having human interactions and not just social media posts! Educating and guiding.

I see many dentists thriving in times of difficulty. Covid and the fear of recession not holding them back. Using systems I have invented, tried and tested, I am seeing my free snazzy marketing and advertising strategies being utilised. And sometimes just hearing how a conversation lightened the load makes my day. Passing on wisdom and experience is the endgame for me. Don't misunderstand me, though – my passion to defend and acquire will always be with me. Take what is mine and I will *want* to punch you in the throat, but a more balanced business approach will follow, not a street fight.

I know my way is not the only way, but it is, instead, another viewpoint, a reassuring hand on the back, a guiding light. I am left humbled by people wanting to hear me talk, hear about my experiences – some good, some bad. I have made some mistakes in my life. If I can share these with others, it may make their paths that bit easier. So, I have booked out courses. We all share and we all learn together. I show how I have built and sold many businesses for millions. All I ask is a day to show you. To see the changes possible. What a difference a day makes.

CHAPTER 3

MISTRUTHS vs THE UGLY TRUTH

We are held back by our beliefs. My therapist told me that right at the start of my journey. 'Trust the process', Grace Chatting used to say. Change your beliefs and change your mindset. Mindset, though, is the most powerful of mental and psychological shifts. Drive in a car. Someone jumps out in front of you ... there's no thought, no conscious process from the brain to the foot. Before you have a chance to shout out 'What the hell!' your foot has hit the brake and you have stopped the car. That is like a mindset-controlled subconscious reaction. Powerful – fast – effective – without thought – without any doubt or objections.

In life we are filled with beliefs and objections. We all carry them in that bag with the dead dog, from our upbringing, our parents, and our parents' parents. Basically, we were screwed the minute we were born. Told not to get too excited, to hold the nerve, to behave, not to shout, not to laugh too loudly. All of these controlled emotions you carry with you for a lifetime. In that bag. That bag is called 'The Shadow'.

I always talk about lighting up the darkness, so in the spirit of lighting up the shadow, I will highlight a few beliefs and objections I have encountered that hold back so many talented dentists. To change a mindset and to make a shift can really make you bust out of your zone of excellence and you will enter your zone of genius. Read *Leap of Faith* by Gay Hendricks. To avoid going too deeply into the psychological processes, I will break down the most common beliefs and objections. You probably won't relate to all of them, you may not relate to any, but think hard and dig deep: you will have beliefs and objections that hold you back from entering your zone of genius. They prevent you from opening that squat, buying that business, converting to private. Whatever the reason, whatever the fear, behind that emotion is always an objection or a belief.

I don't need to get involved. I can just outsource all the marketing.

Yep, I totally understand this. We work in a defined area (the oral cavity) for a defined amount of time in a pool of extreme stress. One slip of the scalpel or drill and we are deep in the mire. I don't think the public appreciates the fine line we tread every time someone opens their mouth. I was out for dinner with a butcher once. He turned round to me and said that he was annoyed because he didn't earn the same money as me. He had a job with a lot of responsibility. He had a job that he had to make sure no one died (poisoned), so why didn't he earn the big money? He said he also played with sharp knives and cut into meat...

I was in pre-therapy and he annoyed me. Defensively, I snapped back, 'Maybe you do cut into meat, but try doing that when the animal is still breathing.' Anyway, I won that argument. So, in short, I appreciate why dentists don't have time to add another responsibility to their list. The sharp knife and the breathing human make the job pretty bloody stressful. The time spent creating adverts and ensuring those adverts are working is just not top of the priority list!

In your defence, you can outsource the marketing but, in my experience, you have to understand what you want. Your passion, your ideas. Expecting another person to create a vision that belongs to you – it feels so alien to me. If you understand what you need, understand your passion and the direction you want to go, then anything is possible. Anyone can help you get there. Outsourcing your marketing with no understanding of yourself is handing over the keys to your business. The owner of the business needs to be in charge of how the marketing cog is fitting in with your branding and unique selling points (USP – something we go into depth about a little later in the book).

But marketing doesn't need to take up much of your time.

You just have to adjust the sails and let the wind take the boat in whatever direction you want. The wind being your marketing agency. Sit back and let the staff run it. You just have to give them direction. Relax in the knowledge that you will have an endless pool of patients ready to sign up to your plan or accept more exciting treatment options. The truth is, if you let the ship sail without you on board, it takes approximately six to twelve months, on average, for a campaign to gain traction and become a successful strategy. Don't you want to do more of the dentistry you love? Marketing done right is the answer. Reduce your hours and select the patients who don't give you that red flag fear. You can even put up your prices as the demand grows. You are the master of your own destiny.

I don't know what I am doing and have no clue where to start.

This is so common; it is a fear that I hear on a daily basis. Dentists will ring up and request for me to design an advert for them. They want me to provide the artwork and edit the copy. It is usually targeting associates for a position they have available, or they want to provide more cosmetic dentistry and would like to target certain demographics and age groups.

We have to start somewhere!

We all have to start somewhere. I will explain how to find your USP later in the book and then you can hang everything off that – you will have direction. As soon as you know how you want to sell something anything is possible. Creating an advert is easy as soon as you are aware of your USP and branding. Of course, there is a basic structure to a post or advert, and that can be found in the *Resource Pack: Task 1.*

I've never had to do any marketing so I never will.

I talked to a massive group of dentists north of the border: The Scottish Dental Study Club. Tariq is the captain of that ship, alongside his amazingly talented wife, Saimah. They have built some machine there, and I owe a lot to them. When they asked me to talk about dentistry and marketing I jumped at the opportunity. It was daunting: a packed house. I spent the first 40 minutes on the toilet. Anyway, I got great feedback. Then I saw it. One person almost ruined my confidence before I had a chance to flourish in the lecturing circuit: 'I have never had to do any marketing so I never will.' Over the years this has stuck with me, not because it hurts my feelings now but because it is such a misguided objection and belief.

Why do I feel so strongly about this?

We are creatures of habit. We are born to live by a routine. Whether in prison or standing on a desert island – we crave routine like a drug. It makes us feel safe. Until we are met with distinct threats. It doesn't matter what that threat may be. It could be a young dentist moving into your area or a squat that has been built next door or in the neighbouring town. Suddenly that routine doesn't feel safe; it no longer feels like home. Many dentists haven't advertised before because they haven't needed to. Dentists are running out of space to build squats. It's challenging to find an empty street without a dental clinic. So where do we set up? Where do I advise clients to start their dream!? The answer – in a town where other dentists are doing a bad job! Where dentists believe they don't need to advertise. I don't mean you have to be a marketing genius. Just try to be the best you can be. If it all fails and someone does better you can rest easy that the better person won. But to have someone take it all away because you couldn't be bothered – that will haunt your dreams for a lifetime. Trust me – I out-marketed a number of competitors over my time. Dog eat dog. Some of them were worthy competitors. It kept me awake at night thinking about ways to outsmart them. It was a game for me. A game I played well and enjoyed.

Remember that the most successful business figures in the dental field are kind and generous but ruthless also. It is that ruthlessness that sets them apart.

To succeed in life, you have to be better than your competitor – and willing to stick your neck out. Happy to just go for it. When dentists phone me and ask for my advice, when they are on their knees as they become aware of a local competitor – a young blood about to set up nearby – my initial response is always the same: welcome to the game. I just thank the lord I am not a part of the game anymore. I am free. I don't need to watch my back anymore – I won that game a long time ago – so I will leave that fight to the company that bought my last and final squat business.

Those hungry dentists are still out there. Stalking their prey. The super associate. They have money, they have ambition, and they will take your legs out without a second thought. It doesn't matter where or how they got their money. They are just super talented and locked and loaded. Please, to all those dentists who are middle aged, get ready for your own Armageddon. Don't live and be ruled by this objection. It will be your undoing.

Marketing and advertising are unprofessional in a medical industry.

This is a very common belief and objection to change. I get it. We aren't selling cheap second-hand crap. We are selling health. I really do think we sell every day, all day. It doesn't matter if we are at home or at work, we need to sell to get what we want. It goes way back. My dad is a retired dentist. In his day the marketing was the gold plate and putting up your plate was the be all and end all. It was considered a proud moment. The defining point in one's career. Placing your name on your wall. It was a complete marketing strategy, and the only strategy. Patients came flocking. They were also allowed to put their name in the phone book. Of course, it was 'Mr' not the 'Dr' title used for surgeons. Hence why dentists were not given the same title as our medical colleagues. (Incidentally, when we advertise we have to make it blatantly clear we are not medical Drs. A joke really: their title is as much an honorary title as ours! The true 'Dr' is a doctorate in philosophy, apparently.)

I believe that one of the reasons there is an objection regarding marketing in the dental world is handed down from our predecessors. It was frowned upon, but my era has started to change that (I qualified in 1997). However, mark my words, there is a new predator: dentists with two degrees or more. Whether they are dual trained in business, law, accountancy, they are emerging. Get ready and brace yourself, or you can retire, of course. Hang up your boots and stand aside. With all this education and knowledge, they will erode into the life you worked so hard to create.

Patients are no longer loyal. They can see price comparisons with the touch of a finger, they can view testimonials and reviews. They can research you without the need to pick up the phone or drive to your practice. In my dad's day, patients had to give you a go and meet you. Try and test what you have to offer. Now it's so much easier to make a decision: compare and contrast. For goodness' sake, you have to get over this objection or it could be a painful lesson. To be fair, I would love to go back to the good old days. I loved the gold plate moment, but I accept those days are long gone.

I also do not understand why it is considered unethical to advertise in dentistry. I just don't see it, and I have never understood the thought process behind it. We see health adverts everywhere. We see osteopaths, chiropractors, private clinics and hospitals. Bupa adverts are commonplace. You can't go anywhere without seeing opticians' adverts (no pun intended). TV campaigns ads, traditional marketing strategies in magazines and papers. Why are dentists so very different? Why do we feel it is beneath us to display our skills to the world through marketing? There are strict rules we must adhere to: be honest, do not be misleading, do not make promises you cannot keep. These guidelines are set down by the GDC. Follow these rules and the Advertising Standards Authority – they make sense. Advertise professionally and you will be regarded as such.

I can't ask my staff to do any more because they are so busy.

My staff are busy enough. How can I get them to do more chores? My extra requests will ruin their day. They will just moan at me. How can I make them do what I ask when a simple request is denied or ignored? My staff are run off their feet – like me, they are chasing their tails, putting out fires.

I appreciate this objection. When I started out in business, trying to organise chaos was a tough uphill struggle! It just felt like I was piling on more crap. Changing habits, changing hearts and minds, is tough, especially when you are alone at the top. Piling more crap on staff is a bit like throwing petrol on the fire. It felt like it would just cause more problems. It was knowing where and how to introduce those systems that meant an easier life for me and not extra work, extra stress and even less free time for me to spend with my family. So, I totally get this objection. How can one extra system make life easier? I remember thinking that making no change was better than the fear of more chaos or worse – failure.

When I have shown dentists a system it isn't in isolation. It is a gentle approach to the entire patient journey. An easy way to ensure your marketing follows through to reception, booking the patient in, conversion techniques and finally testimonial collection and patient retention. On average, I had 200 new patients a month seated in the dental chairs and ready to discuss treatment. That comes about by establishing a patient journey that everyone can manage, using tips and tricks the entire business can apply and appreciate – why? Because it makes their lives easier and not more complicated. All this stuff – all this dental business stuff – it ain't rocket science.

We will address this later in the book. I will show you how to organise reception, selling your vision to the staff in a way that will ensure that they will get on board and help you steer the business through choppy seas. (Choppy seas could mean anything: a new super associate is setting up next door, you are unable to work for a time, an associate goes off long-term sick, you get a GDC investigation, a staff member takes you to an industrial tribunal…)

Those who quietly go about their day, refraining from posting their material wealth, are the ones to look towards to model a more peaceful and better organised business.

More dentists + more staff = higher turnover = more profit, so I have no time for all this!

It takes huge courage to step back from the dental chair. From drilling teeth. It takes courage to loosen the grip and pay someone else to do the treatments you could be doing. When I started out, the more work I did the more I grossed, and the more profit I made. That was my mantra and, of course, the 'more, more, more' strategy does lead to burnout and exhaustion. How bloody soul destroying. It was a painful lesson when I discovered that my life had become quite empty. It was just work, but I can make this promise: it will all be worth it, as, when everything is running smoothly, you can start to enjoy all the other areas of your life as well as your day job!

To step back a bit, reducing the hours takes courage. I appreciate that we all live within our means. So, the more you have earned, the more you have spent. Therefore, to pay someone else seems like a ludicrous action. I can promise you something, though: you will gross more working a four-

---

**You will gross more
working a four-day week
than a five.**

---

day week than a five. That one day recharges your batteries, allowing you time to reflect and sharpen the senses. You have more energy and enthusiasm and (I forgot to mention!) a free clinic to get another clinician in to expand your growing business.

This belief is all too common. I have experienced the relief of the four-day week shift. My only regret is that I never made the shift sooner in my career.

The GDC is out to get us.

The GDC. I could write an entire book about my experiences at the hands of the GDC. I remember my first investigation. To be honest it wasn't even an investigation; a few poorly chosen words from a colleague to a patient of mine resulted in the regulator asking for their notes. I felt my world had caved in overnight. That and discretionary indemnity cover helped me to come to realise, one Sunday morning, that to s*** yourself was not purely a mental phenomenon.

Yep, I sharted. My nerves had taken that much of a battering. How can a job be that stressful? Looking back, I realised that both experiences with the GDC were terrifying. But the fear was all self-generated. The actual process was relatively painless. When I say painless, it did have its ups and downs, but I had two very supportive specialist orthodontists in my corner. Firstly – Dr. Ramtin Taheri, I will always be grateful to him. A real gem. Kind, clever, and a bloody good businessman. Ruthless as well! And of course, the IAS Professor Ross Hobson. He scared the crap out of me but is a superb teacher. I can safely say these particular specialist orthodontists came to my rescue more than once! And Dr. Hobson's teaching changed the way I did dentistry and taught me how orthodontics should be done. No shortcuts, no compromises. When I started, a weekend course was all that was necessary to 'shuffle teeth' – I still have the words of the prof echoing in my ears 'You don't know what you don't know'. I can safely say after a clear aligner weekend course – I knew bugger all! And I didn't know I knew bugger all.

Do the job right and you have nothing to fear from the GDC. Or the legal eagles. The GDC is there for a reason. To protect the public. To investigate. Regulators are never very popular with any profession but they are there to regulate. I really do want to position them as fair and balanced – but only in my experience.

I have heard some horror stories, however. I remember seeing some hard facts. How many dentists do they strike off? It is quite sobering. It isn't that many. We have just created a monster image of the GDC on social media. There are a number of dentists who encourage colleagues to pay the regulatory fees late and challenge the GDC with numerous legal threats. A little secret – the GDC are not running scared. They don't find it intimidating. They just tot up the hours and charge them back to us.

Death, taxes and the third one – regulation. All jobs worldwide are now subject to heavy regulations and restrictions. We are not any different. I have a mate called Martin Thornton. A GP. True story! I've known him for years. He became a CQC inspector and, in his words, he loved visiting dentists. We were the easiest, most polite, most accommodating out of all the medical professions. We have created this fear of regulators within the profession. I do blame social media, and I blame the profession we chose. Not because it isn't a great job, but because there isn't an alternative if we lost the ability to drill teeth. Not an alternative that would give us the same financial benefits we have come to know and appreciate. Having the possibility of it being taken away – that is the fear we lie awake contemplating.

> *My best day in dentistry was just tolerable,*
> *my worst day as a lorry driver was tolerable.*

That is a quote I heard from a mate who gave up dentistry. Sometimes that fear – that stress – can just be so overwhelming. Would I choose to do dentistry if I was 18 again? For sure. When I graduated it was in the midst of the golden years: easy dentistry with no regulations and litigation uncommon. Would I encourage my children? I am just glad I am not having to make that decision. They want to go into finance and politics/media and history.

We do worry about our businesses – we worry we will be sued by staff, associates, patients – and this can zap so much energy out of us. It is energy we could put to use expanding, developing and improving systems and operations within the business. We worry that if we put our head above the parapet, the GDC will have us in their sights and local colleagues will think negatively about us. I do understand this fear. Just don't be the last person to enter the game.

> *I have a very stable patient base, so I don't need to bother*
> *with marketing.*

The practice plans and payment options have helped stabilise patient lists. It's a bit like the gym. They stick with one place so there is less of a necessity to market for new patients. Many dental practices have a monthly turnover from Denplan payments. They were laughing when Covid hit. Fee per item practices struggled far more. However, saying that, patient habits are changing and buying habits are becoming more transient. They may go to one place for an implant, another for Invisalign. They may have an NHS practice for their check-ups. The truth is we need new patients to come through the door despite the method you have adopted to retain the old ones. A business needs new mouths that aren't stable. New mouths that will spread the word about how amazing you are. If you solely rely on monthly plans, I do think this could be a mistake waiting to happen. 20 years ago, the patient had to visit the surgery to see if you were any good. Now they just jump on Google My Business.

I hope I have demonstrated that we are all very similar. We all struggle with the same beliefs and objections. And fears! We have probably all struggled over the years. I have known the hardest of men crying at the thought of a GDC hearing. But dentistry is a beautiful profession; it allows the artist within us to flourish, the businessman to flex their muscles, the healer to heal. However, it does have its downside too. It can be hard, stressful, gruelling. We struggle the same and experience the same stresses. But if we can somehow recognise that objections and beliefs can hold us back, letting them go and advancing forward, developing the business and making life easier for ourselves can be not only exciting but life changing.

Dental Defence Organisations 'The Ugly Truth' – will they dump me if I start advertising?

For 25 years I have been in the trade. I have used many different indemnity providers for different businesses. From feet to teeth, from the business of dentistry to clinical dentistry. And one fact is clearly obvious – there is much confusion about this topic. So here it is: 'the Ugly Truth' – My Truth.

Let me provide a simple example. If my wife crashed into my car (this happened once!) in a supermarket car park, I wouldn't expect my house insurance to cover this. Point one made. Our indemnity cover is for clinical dentistry. I am not sure why this is confusing. I see many posts about dentists in distress about some legal issue that is unrelated to the actual drilling of teeth. They then get multiple online messages recommending a call to their indemnity company. So here is the ugly truth – it won't help if unrelated to clinical dentistry and why should it? Our indemnity providers are not there to provide a blanket insurance cover for every Tom, Dick & Harry who wants to sue us.

Point two is the 'discretionary cover' policy. Have you noticed all these new companies springing up? 'We provide super cover. We will do better than the big four. Oh, by the way, we also have a discretionary policy'. This policy seemed to spring up overnight. All the major companies suddenly started adding it to their T&Cs. There are a number of reasons this was an unwanted addition to the policy in my opinion. For one, it protects the companies from dentists wanting to use their indemnity against their wives crashing into them in the supermarket car park! It also protects them from the Harold

Shipman-type multiple claims. Can you imagine if 500 claims came through all at once from one dentist? It would cripple the organisation. The way some lawyers post their wins in the local newspaper and encourage others to come forward with similar claims – this is a highly probable scenario! Do I agree with this policy? I think it is a necessary evil. I had an issue with my house a year ago. Insurance based. They refused my cover because of the small print. So not all insurance-based cover is a 100% safe blanket of love and protection!

And finally, to the point we have all been waiting for. Point three: 'Will they dump me?' Like I said – 25 years in the trade. Life is all about cycles. Frank Sinatra song! An old friend sent me this. Great song. Anyway, back to the point. Dentistry is no different. When I started a couple of decades ago it was considered the golden years. We could do anything. I could do 12 unit bridges on the NHS and multiple crown preparations without any form of note-taking. I remember looking back and seeing my exam notes in 2001 – Exam S&P. Now they are two pages long. Dentistry had to change. But that change came with a sense of panic. Change and fear go hand in hand. The indemnity providers got twitchy. The GDC got twitchy. I remember the term 'defensive dentistry'. The first time I heard it. It took a while to spread to the rolling hills of Devon from London. Like a whisper in the wind. I thought it was describing the dentist's attitude as being defensive because the patients were being ungrateful! How naive was I? It was around the time of the suing culture at its most extreme. The golden years of dentistry were gone for good. The public was suddenly suing everyone. From stomach issues on holiday to PCP agreements, to Land Rover emissions. I remember my wife was offered

£1200 for inappropriate advice provided by a bank relating to a loan taken out years previous. It was literally a phone call away! The world had gone mad! Back to dentistry. The GDC paid for an advert to be placed in a major newspaper. The profession was up in arms. It went crazy. I have to say I totally understand the frustration. The article was not about encouraging patients to complain to the GDC, it was about the new service – The Dental Complaints Service. By the way, if you get a complaint I would prefer this bunch to investigate it! It was just a poorly thought-out and badly designed article. Regardless, society had hit a new level of crazy and with any change there has to be an adjustment. Who would have taken the hit with these changes? The indemnity providers and the GDC. And of course, the dental team providing the treatment.

In the last ten years, I have seen hundreds of posts about moving indemnity cover purely down to a cost saving. I want to clear something up for the record. You cannot compare apples with pears. I will now try to explain why – for the record. Let us take the DDU. I have been with them for 20 years. Through the ups and downs. During the golden years to the panic of defensive dentistry and through to what I would call a period of calm. They provide a cover called Claims Occurring. That means when I am on my boat retired and Mrs. Smith returns to the practice and complains about the crap crown I fitted 20 years ago, the DDU would pick up the claim and sort it out as long as I was covered by them during the time of the incident. Make sense? So that is like a lifelong cover, and with this promise you expect it to be more expensive. The other cover, Claims Made insurance. Mrs. Smith returns after 20 years to complain about the crown. If you do not have 'Run Off' cover this retirement boat trip gets somewhat more stressful. I tried to leave my facial aesthetics insurance cover. Run off is costing me! I took the insurance out in case some patient makes a complaint about me for some eye lift I provided 10 years ago. I can see this cover will get expensive!

So there it is. Hopefully, that makes sense now. Do not compare different types of covers. You can't compare car prices if they are different cars. Make sure you know what you are paying for.

Point three (final point) – did the DDU dump me? What I can say is the DDU has supported me for 20 years. They will not pay out if they don't need to. For the last six years they have fought tooth and nail (excuse the pun) and managed to get both cases thrown out. Why did they fight? Because they had an argument. There is no point fighting the good fight if the case would most likely fall at the last hurdle. Damage limitation. I want to give a special shout-out to Emma Gilroy and Alison Large – you are both superstars! To sum it up, I would never leave the DDU; they really are supportive and will fight 'if' they can.

So if you are considering indemnity, I would definitely have a chat with the DDU, I would make sure I fully grasped the different types of cover, and I would try to stay off Facebook and not use it as a source of information!

So hopefully that sums up clinical negligence cover. Now back to the show.

CHAPTER 4

MY APPROACH – THE STFD BUSINESS MODEL

Strategic Tree For Dentists

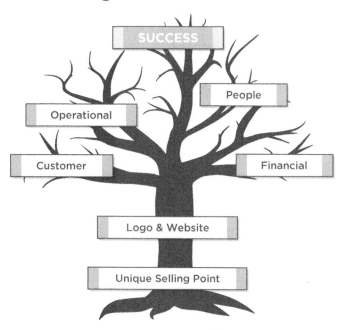

My STFD. A business development model for dentists. It has everything you will ever need to run and grow your business. It stands for:

Strategic
Tree
For
Dentists.

I mention it at the many courses I run. I always get a few smiles and laughs from the mavericks who appreciate the humour, others furiously scribble away.

When I started out, I just wanted something to cool down my boiling pot of disorganisation. I was floating around putting out fires, with no direction or a reference point, until I sat down one night and put pen to paper. I wanted one page, one easy-to-understand flow diagram. I have lived a very interesting life and met some fascinating people: from being on *Baywatch*, meeting Julia Roberts, having a long conversation with Robin Williams, to being kicked off a film set by Steven Spielberg, I can safely say I have met a fair few heavy hitters! However, developing my STFD business model and discussing it with some people far cleverer than I goes down as one of my greatest and most rewarding achievements.

So, what is it? If I had to summarise, it is a tree diagram representing everything that must be spot on in your business for it to survive and grow.

The roots

The Unique Selling Point, I can safely say (and with confidence), is the most important part of the tree. It's the roots. It's where the growth happens, and it provides all the resources for all the branches of the tree.

That's it! Easy.

The main branches of the tree are as follows:

1. Operational – We will focus on the cogs and wheels here. Easy to implement free tools & strategies that will make life easier for you and your staff. Your processes will be seamless.

2. People – We will examine how you treat your staff, what you expect from them, and of course, what they can expect from you. This will mean running through how you can make sure your team works as a team and not a cage of lions.

3. Customer – We will cover how you can make a five-star reception team without having to pay for loads of training. Easy tips and tricks will mean that your staff will be like a posh hotel concierge team!

4. Financial – We will look at how you can keep the wolves from the door, discussing tips and tricks that will supercharge your business

So, there it is. My STFD business model. I even added a cute little PDF diagram of the tree in the *Resource Pack: Task 2*, so you can visualise it and develop your business using an easy-to-follow structure. Just remember, though, that this stuff – all this dental business stuff – ain't rocket science. This business model can be used for your interviews, contracts and disciplinaries. I put together a mind-blowing employees' contract with the above subheadings. Everything was in it: staff respecting each other (People), treating customers with a smile (Customer), collecting deposits (Financial) and even small but vital parts of the business, like how and when to book patients in (Operational) and much more. If the staff push back, get the big guns in. Peninsula were a welcome addition to my team. They adapted the contracts, managed out irritating staff and insured me if any of the staff fancied their chances in court. Head over to the *Resource Pack: Task 3* to get a contract review, a 1-2-1 HR Consultation and a Compliance Health Check with Phil Clark from Peninsula – all for free since you have bought this book! He will have a look at your contractual arrangements to see where you have a weakness in the chain.

I finally started to control the business. I could see it on one easy diagram that grew with the business. It wasn't static. Staff helped it come alive. When a staff member came in with thongs that poked out over their hipsters – or tattoos plastered over their arms – I just added it to the relevant part of the tree (after a quick chat with HR). Clear and concise and, above all, it offered controlled reactions with no knee-jerk responses.

So, what is the outcome of embracing the STFD business model? It is a complete holistic plan to grow your business all in one neat little diagram; it's easy to understand, easy to develop and grow, easy to see from a distance. It's a business model that will grow with you and your staff, from disciplinary procedures to bonuses. It encompasses the dental business from start to finish.

So, why does my tree work?

Reason 1: It cuts through the noise and gives you a simple plan

I needed something that I could just look at and not get drowned in the complexity of all the processes we see online. The STFD approach works holistically. Remember the chain? If one part is broken, then we bleed our finances. No point increasing marketing when the reception drops the baton. There is no point training reception when the dentists are unable to convert patients. The business has to be considered as a whole. It has to be viewed as one complete entity. Make small improvements across the board and you will see massive gain. Train one area and you will see more losses as the area you are trying to improve will snap under the pressure. I was tired of introducing strategies that got dropped when others were introduced. If someone gave me paperwork and numbers, I got stressed – still do. I feel anxious, as the words on the page look dead to me. Revising for me was a nightmare. Again, balance – find what you are good at and make it work for you. If you solve problems in isolation, it becomes stressful, confusing and staff will lose patience, so I initially just made this complete strategy for myself. To ease the burden of running a business and to regain control. The

STFD business model is a complete strategy that develops with you and your business.

Reason 2: It's about your whole business

I look at a business like a long chain. No matter how strong that chain is, it is only as strong as the weakest link. If you throw loads of money at a marketing strategy and the receptionists fail to nurture the lead – or worse, fail to pick up the bloody phone – it won't be long before you feel like going on Facebook and writing a crappy testimonial claiming your marketer feeds you with rubbish leads. In my honest opinion, there is no such thing as a bad lead! Just poorly nurtured enquiries. I also think advertising and marketing are based a lot on luck. We do make our own luck, but as soon as you know how to post a paid advert on Facebook there is no reason why you can't do this yourself. (If you want to learn that is!) If you don't want to do it yourself, pay someone else! *The funny thing about a diagram is the completeness you get from it. You see where it is lacking. You may have too many customer strategies and forget the people. There may be a severe lack of attention to the financial aspects of the business. As soon as you see it in one easy diagram you can add to it and let it grow and develop.*

Reason 3: It becomes part of the fabric of your business, making everything easier

In the days of my squat builds, I regularly put up the STFD poster in the staff room. Staff would add to it if they felt they didn't have a voice. If someone was cruel or two-faced, they would add a one-liner under 'People', the rest of the staff would get the message and change their attitude. It became alive. It became a part of the team. It gave a voice to the quieter team members. I could just add to it and it didn't feel like a knee-jerk reaction. If I witnessed a staff member passing a patient without saying hello, or a receptionist forgetting to ask a patient's name, this could be added to the tree. When I felt that 'Oh damn, that was awful. How am I going to deal with it?' moment, I just added it onto the tree. It was almost cleansing. I would add it to the 'Customer' branch. If I noticed deposits weren't being taken when patients were booking in, I would add a one-liner 'Staff must take deposits' under 'Financial'. If we had a new enquiry, the reception team had to add the details onto our CRM system. If this was not happening, the request would be placed under 'Operational'. The tree – my tree – came alive. I remember the first time a staff member added their bit – their requests – it was some moment for me. I realised it was working. It became part of the team. I suppose it was a worry board, but it had an impact!

Reason 4: It gets quick and dramatic results

My point is that a dental business has many branches. There are so many areas where the baton can be dropped, so improve all of the areas a little and the business will grow at an enormous rate that you never thought was possible. I went from a gross turnover of £300k to £1.7 million in the space of 15 months when I started thinking about the business as a whole. Thinking of it as a tree. The STFD business model. This year we hit our £2 million T/O target with a small 1,200 sq. ft building in a sleepy Devon town – I am very proud of these results. We also respond to over 250 enquiries and booked in over 200 new patients a month. This system works – I have taught others to utilise the STFD business model, and the results have been fantastic. I have built many squats and businesses over my career, but my proudest moment was realising my STFD business model was transferrable. I realised it was possible to pass it onto others and they would also benefit from it. When you get to the crossroads of your career, passing on experience is like no other feeling: a moment of pride. Writing this book and sharing this system with you will always stay with me as being one of my proudest moments in my career.

Reason 5: It makes running a business less stressful

I remember that when I started out building practices I had no clue how to run a business. I didn't realise there should be a plan or a strategy. If you use the STFD business model you can share your energy around the different areas of the business. You can see which areas of the business you have been working on and other areas that need developing. It is a visual bird's eye view of your business on one page! Make life easier for yourself.

When we start out, all we think about is getting the patients through the door. More patients, more teeth, more money, less stress. Well, in the short term this approach does offer less stress, as the bank manager is kept happy, but (as we will see later in the book) it can grind you down if working this way is not kept carefully managed and carefully monitored. At the start of any of the squat practices I built in the early days, the customer list (Advertising branch) was as long as your arm. That was all I focused on. It was also probably why I lost so many members of staff over a six-month period; I forgot about the most important part of the business: the staff. The People branch of the model.

Who it works for

Regardless of your history, no matter how intelligent you are or when you started your dental business, this system will work for you, making your life that little bit easier and bringing control to your business. The system will grow itself; you just need to trust your staff and yourself. You just have to hold the nerve, dig deep and take a leap of faith. Change comes with fear, just don't forget to breathe and that fear can turn into excitement. You will see a new you, a less stressful you. You will look forward to work rather than fearing that foggy weight that hangs around your neck. I know that foggy feeling. That constant hum of stress and anxiety. So, let's start living and not just surviving. Trust me and join me on this journey.

So, who can use the STFD business model? Anyone. No matter how far along the journey you are. No matter where your dreams are going to take you. It will just help you to grow. Help you to maintain a healthy level of control and allow the business to grow with you. If you are tired and exhausted, it really will relieve the burden. If you are firing on all cylinders and riding on the crest of a wave, it will give you that bird's eye view of the business and you can develop it to suit your needs. It is the complete business package, developed by a dentist for dentists.

We all need results, that is human nature, but we want to make sure we are safe before we put any effort in. We are being reviewed even before patients come through the door. If you take anything away from this book, start building reviews and testimonials. If you want to stay in a hotel, you always check out what other people have said about their experiences. You want to know your hard-earned cash is being spent well. It's true the world over. It's me, it's your patients, and so I totally appreciate you wanting to know this system works and your valuable time isn't wasted before you put any effort in! First things first. I have built many squat practices, and other businesses outside dentistry, and it has worked for me and many clients I have mentored. I appreciate that dentists do love case studies, so here is one of the many success stories I have had the pleasure of being a part of.

I was contacted a year ago by a very well-known dentist. They asked me to improve their business, offering me a substantial monthly sum, but it just didn't feel right. An already successful dentist known by everyone. Known by you, I can assure you. So, I picked up the phone and contacted the practice, a cosmetic practice.

The lovely lady picked up the phone and I asked about the price of their veneers. 'Oh, I wouldn't do veneers as they damage your teeth. Why don't you do braces with whitening and some bonding?' I had to pick myself up off the floor. Veneers were a large part of that particular dentists' treatment options. They may be more destructive than align, bleach and bond but it was not the receptionist's job to advise me on the subject, especially when it contradicted advice that could have been given on consultation. The lovely lady didn't ask me my name, asked me no questions, didn't ask me where I had heard of the business. A train wreck. Yes, she was nice but there was no panache, no sparkle. I have a set form I fill out when I carry out mystery shops (see the resources page). Show them the form and say that you will be testing them once a week. That's usually enough to put a rocket under their chairs.

I went back to the lead dentist. I said that throwing money at the business would not solve the issue, so we put together a plan. It took three hours. I showed them the STFD strategy. How to establish their USP through the processes used at the reception and a couple of operational techniques, customer care tips and tricks. Small changes across the board = massive results. The hole in the bucket was repaired. The extra effort and, if necessary, extra finances would be put to good use someplace else.

Another example was a dentist who was drowning in enquiries, North East England. They simply couldn't cope. The gross turnover did not reflect the level of demand they were experiencing. There were no systems in place. We looked at the 'Operational' arm of the tree. We introduced automation, which in turn relieved the admin team to develop the business in other key areas. We looked at the 'Patient' area and discovered that the associates (particularly one of them) had the most consultations yet the lowest conversion rates. Decisions were made to train that dentist. New patients were shared out and the gross went up. I think that the biggest killer in business is a lack of accountability. Introduce that and anything is possible. The STFD business model allows this to be introduced. It gets you to see what is going on and where, and it allows you to see where you are bleeding. My North East England dentist had an issue with associate conversions. It was assessed, diagnosed and a plan was put in place.

The biggest killer in business is a lack of accountability.

The most common issue is that 'my marketing firm is providing rubbish leads'. I probably receive this on a weekly basis. As the economy pinches, this issue will become even more common. When I get this feedback, I pull out the STFD business model diagram and take note of how the dentist incorporates structure into the business. The usual answer is that there is little structure, if any at all.

How can you assess your marketer when you fail to record how many enquiries you get? How can you assess the quality of the leads when conversion rates are not monitored? How can you criticise anyone when the phones aren't answered, deposits aren't taken, emails aren't answered? The answer is you can't. **If all these systems and operations are not in place, then you are driven by feeling.** You have a feeling the marketing firms are not doing their job. Feeling has no place in calculating the numbers. Gut instinct is always a powerful tool, but when the gut instinct shows up solid evidence it has to be investigated before you can pick up the phone and fall out with your marketer.

Falling out with a trusted marketer can be a painful lesson. They can turn your world upside down, remove all of your marketing strategies that were doing well, leaving you with a business that is worthless. I have actually seen this happen. A dentist from the southwest. I felt sorry for them. They blamed their marketer (who subsequently deleted all the campaigns and refused to work with them) for crap leads. Then they discovered the reception team never picked up the phone – they actually routinely let the call go to the answer machine. But this wasn't all. Their associate was stealing from them. It went unnoticed. There was just zero control – zero accountability – and it was everybody else's fault.

These are not isolated stories. I have changed many dentists' lives, and the one person I am particularly proud of – myself. I saved myself and my family by regaining control of my business and, therefore, making my life easier. I increased my gross by making my staff accountable, and I stopped worrying all the time. I created a strategy, one strategy, to have an easier life. Through the STFD business model that became possible.

In short, the STFD business model gives you a clear system to look at, evaluate and improve every 'branch' of your business, from what's happening in reception to what's happening in the staff and consultation rooms. That bird's eye view is key!

If you have this structure, then you can build on it and allow it to develop with your growing business. Every dental surgery is different, but we all need firm roots. We all need to consider each branch of the tree. When your head is down in their mouths, the approach can get cloudy and the business can get lost. The tree allows us to be brought back to the important parts of the business and allows others to get involved in the development. If you are still with me, can you go a little further? Trust me a little while longer. I appreciate time is the most precious commodity we all have, but it will be the best investment you will ever make. It could literally change your life. I appreciate change is tough, change is hard and change is scary. I read a quote the other day, and it's the best quote I have ever heard:

Anything worth having lies just beyond the boundary of fear! Keep going!

What a very cool saying. I love change. I remember my mum used to say a change is as good as a rest. It allows you time to reflect, to move on with different stages of your life. I have changed my life every four years. I won't change my wife, just everything else. I have built houses, businesses, squat practices, inventions. You name it, I have done it – but if you have structure, when faced with the need for a change, it becomes that much easier. That structure I will explain to you in the next few chapters.

I am in the process of introducing the STFD business model to other businesses outside the dental world. The tree is just a structure, an easy way of looking at the whole business, but it turns into a strategy when you put the meat on the bones, so allow it to grow. It is a constant reminder to return to what is important in the business, to remind you to go back to your roots. Find your 'why', your uniqueness, and, in doing so, you will confirm your unique selling point – what separates you from the wolves down the street.

So here goes. I hope you embrace it; I want to introduce you to a life-changing plan, so say hello to the STFD business model.

CHAPTER 5

UNIQUE SELLING POINT

Colleagues just love criticising dentists for making a commodity out of the dental profession. How some loathe the open day deals and low-cost Invisalign prices being splashed across Facebook. I think they find it an insult to the profession, making it look cheap. Whilst I don't necessarily agree, I do think that there are 35,000 dentists in the UK and all of them are doing the same old thing. Advertising Invisalign, dental implants, facial aesthetics and now cosmetic bonding. I discovered that cosmetic bonding is a more popular Google search term than Invisalign! This may or may not be true but what it does show me is that we are all fishing in the same pond! We are all scrapping over the same pool of patients! We need to start thinking outside the box; we need to be different and we need to find our unique qualities that will encourage patients to choose us over the competitor. I do think today's marketing strategies are so similar: same offer, different place.

So, what makes you unique?

That's where we need to start, but it's something a lot of dentists struggle with. That's why on all my courses dentists come up to me in the break and ask for help discovering their USP. They want to stand out from the crowd. They want to be noticed. They want to discover what makes them unique. They want to look inside themselves to discover what makes them special. Without that, they don't have a hope of communicating a USP.

People talk about finding out their 'why', but I find it a bit flowery. To ask someone their why is not an easy discussion. Why do they go to work? Why do they do dentistry? Why do they want to provide cosmetic dentistry or provide dental treatment to nervous patients?

Whenever I chat through with dentists about their why, it is always quite tough to establish. We just weren't taught this stuff. We got our degree, we opened our shops, and off we went. So, your patterns of behaviour, your drive and the reasons you do many daily tasks are at a subconscious level. You just do them. Well, this is the area of your mind where you will find your why, just beneath the surface, so it can take a little digging.

The way you find your unique selling point is linked to your uniqueness, that, in turn, is related to and linked to your passions.

PASSION – UNIQUENESS – UNIQUE SELLING POINT

When I support a new business, I ask them to look at their competitors, but that is always secondary to digging deep into their souls to locate their passion and, in the process, their uniqueness.

So, what is a unique selling point? It is what sets you apart from everyone else. It is what makes Google better than Yahoo. It is what makes the Apple phone better than Nokia. **Your unique selling point is what delivers your unique message to the world** – to your potential patients. The vehicle. It is the essence of what makes you stand taller and better than your competitor.

If I was to be blunt and define USP, I would say that it is the marketing statement you use to sell your products and services to prospective customers, but it is linked to your unique qualities as a person. It can't be plucked from a hat and created in response to another dentist who has arrived on your street. It isn't about offering a service because others are not. It has to be a part of you to really express the meaning to your potential clients. When your passion and uniqueness are found, you can then shape your USP and create a message that no one in the neighbourhood is offering. It could be opening hours, or it could be the patients' journey. If someone then copies you, you can make the decision: do better or shift your USP. Your uniqueness hasn't changed, you have just changed the direction without changing the overall feel and direction of the business.

YOU CAN NEVER CHANGE YOUR UNIQUENESS BUT YOU CAN SHIFT IT TO SUIT YOUR NEEDS. IF SOMEONE DOES SOMETHING SIMILAR EITHER CHANGE YOURS OR DO BETTER!

'A race to the bottom.' Ashley Latter coined the phrase, but now every dentist uses it. It's very clever actually. How many other marketers have managed to coin a phrase that has lasted for decades? That should make him feel very proud! I understand it to mean that if a local competitor reduces their prices, then you try to match it and sometimes go one step further and reduce yours again. This is obviously met with a similar strategy until you are both providing free treatment! Cain and Abel!

So set your fees and stick to them! I do think this saying will go down in history. If a dentist does enter a price war, they are allowing another business to dictate their focus and plans. This can be soul destroying. This type of battle will keep you awake at night. If you are wondering how I know so much about this... it was me. When I started out, I raced to be the most affordable, the biggest, the best. Can cheap and best exist in harmony? I think it can, but we will approach that later.

I regularly used price as a marketing strategy but didn't link it to my passion. I just entered that race to the bottom. For now, I can safely say I was lost when it came to setting fees as I started out. No sense of uniqueness, no focus, no hook to hang my marketing coat from. I made foolish decisions without thought. I employed equally untalented people that equally had no direction. Looking back, the problem was me, not them. It was my responsibility to show them the way, to show them my way. Did I screw everything up? No! But I can safely say my life could have been easier, more joyful and more fulfilling, and I could have been a lot richer! Money – it is a dirty word, but it is important to have a firm grasp on how to make some or the bank will take everything away from you!

My story

I think it is important to link your past with the present, going back in time to see how your early years shaped you so you can understand the influences others had on your outlook. Part of my story began at boarding school, which is where I developed that fire in my belly, that defensive trait. I saw some horrible things back in boarding school, but I had some equally hilarious times. Many of those moments are probably not suitable for this book.

Day one: the shower. The older boys found it amusing to tuck their testicles and penis back through their legs and waddle around the showers. That was an introduction to how things were going to be. I remember not knowing whether to laugh or cry. Boys had their shampoo spiked. This was the name given to the fine art of peeing in someone's shampoo without the person knowing.

However, every action has an opposite reaction. The reaction to bullying was that someone always pushed back. I remember some younger boarders stole the seniors' margarine. They removed the contents of the tub and took a dump in the base of it before covering it up with margarine and placing it back in the fridge. It would have taken the bully weeks to discover the turd hiding under the margarine waiting to expose its ugly head. How disgusting. The bullying I experienced and the friendships that I made sculpted me into a very passionate human being. In fact, it filled me with all sorts of passions!

This brings me on to the five passions in life! There are five.

To feel, to bond, to learn, to acquire and to defend.

If anyone tries to take what is mine, my passion to defend takes over. If someone is loyal to me, that is more important than anything. I see fair play and choice as a birthright. All of my experiences shaped me and my outlook – they were the building blocks. I just didn't know this when I started out. I just made decisions that felt right but I didn't understand what was behind those decisions. When I realised my values, when I realised what made me unique, I started to build my life around them. My business had a focus and I found my why.

So how did finding my passion and uniqueness help me? When you work out your why it is a lightbulb moment. You find your core belief. The more you become aware, the more you explore what is under the surface of your psyche and you no longer behave in a way you don't understand. There are fewer moments where you feel you were out of order, or rude, or behaved out of character. When you get to know yourself, your uniqueness (the prerequisite to your USP) it helps you understand yourself. You can then question your feelings rather than your feelings ruling the roost. When I found my uniqueness, I was able to appreciate team members and how they were different to me and not be irritated by them. I chose the patients I wanted to treat more wisely. My adverts were focused on my uniqueness and passion rather than clutched from thin air, or someone else's thin air! If I could give you one benefit of finding your unique selling point, then it's 'direction'. It gives you a clearer pathway.

So, what's my USP (my vehicle to share my uniqueness)? I don't give two craps if you are black, white, gay, straight – everybody should have a choice. From my time at boarding school, I grew up wanting to defend my patch. I wanted to have a choice. I questioned everything. I wanted to be told all the information so I could make an informed decision. I supported and protected the people in my life like a caged animal. My strapline was 'To be informed and to have the choice' and I plastered it all over my adverts.

Boarding school was quite restricting. Your milk would be stolen, your lunch would be eaten by the older boys. It gave me a passion to acquire, to build something of my own that couldn't be taken away. I therefore advertised some cost-cutting treatments, not a race to the bottom. I didn't give a damn what others were charging. I charged what I wanted and probably irritated the entire neighbourhood. Did I care? Not really.

'To be informed and to have the choice' is as dull as ditchwater. But it worked, and it still does. My prices reflected my core belief. I sold crowns from £300 to £1,100. They are all different – the patients were given all the information to choose the crown they wanted. I opened Saturdays to give my patients choice. I opened in two locations close by so patients could make further choices. I consciously employed both female and male dentists to allow further choice of clinicians. Why? Because everyone in life, no matter who you are, deserves information to make an informed choice.

When I discovered what made me unique, my passion, I realised why I warmed to certain staff, avoided certain associates. It explained why I found myself happy to chat to some of my employees yet avoid others like the plague. Avoiding staff – for me, I had tried to avoid staff for most of my career. I would put the dental chair back, put my music on and lose time whenever I had to avoid lunchtime gatherings.

I just wanted peace. When I discovered what made me tick, I found I could actually meet and enjoy their company.

I managed to subdue that side of me that just got annoyed with staff that didn't have the same passion, ideals or drive as myself. When you know your why it is not unconscious any longer, and you can control those internal dialogues. You no longer have those thoughts in your head, like reaching out and slapping that ridiculous idiot in the staffroom who spouts crap and treats others with utter contempt.

I will show you how to find your passion, and from there we will go on to how you shape your unique selling point!

What's this step all about?

UPS – Unique Selling Point. It is what separates you from the rest. It certainly is a difficult process to establish a unique selling point in dentistry. We all do teeth. Around 35,000 dentists doing pretty much the same thing, so how on earth can we all be unique? How can we all have a USP? Can two people have the same USP? In my opinion, they certainly cannot, as it wouldn't make them unique. For me it goes deeper. If you find what sets you aside from another person (two people can't be the same) and you hang all your marketing from that vision, then you will establish your own USP. It is about your why and not what. For example, it may have the same language as another dentist, e.g. 'We open 7 days a week'. Two dentists may advertise this as their USP, but it is the reasoning behind their decision to open 7 days a week that is important. One could be that the dentist has always felt restricted in life and wants to offer choice to everyone; a pattern that may not be just related to dentistry but also their life away from the operating chair. For the other, it could be associated with a deep-seated passion to never appear lazy or relaxing and enjoying time off. They are the same message but the why behind the message makes it unique, and so the marketing message is their USP.

Don't get me wrong, many businesses won't go this deep. They won't look inside themselves to find their uniqueness and will, instead, splash out for an advert that makes them different in their area. Their message will relate to cost, gentle dentistry, clean environment, modern equipment, but the reason why these so often fail is the advert is not expressing their passion. In reality, most patients expect all of the above when they visit the dentist. It is a USP without soul, without thought. Have you ever wondered why some businesses thrive and others fail? Apple phones, Google, massive corporations – please don't tell me it is just because they put out a message saying 'we offer what others don't'. They have searched for their why, so set yourselves apart from the rest and find your why!

Your why: the reason you go to work, the reason you make decisions. It is a part of you. The funny thing is it is why you make all your decisions. Well, the ones that fit anyway. You know the decisions that don't quite feel right. It could be a new staff member, an advert, a business decision; it's when you get that uneasy feeling. This feeling is either fear or the decision you have made is not in line with your uniqueness and passion. If you have a passion 'to learn', get out and start showing people how clever you are; employ motivated staff who also want to learn, start blogging, start showing your worth. Stop putting out open day deals that irritate more than inspire you.

Don't get me wrong, I have a deep passion to acquire. This is the one passion that has to be balanced. I see many Facebook posts when dentists show off their wealth, cars and houses. There are 'well dones' and 'congratulations'. Reality check: 99% of readers are slating you for showing off. It may be jealousy, but the passion to acquire (acquiring wealth, status, toys) can be a painful pathway, a lonely one, so get it balanced.

For me, with the passion to acquire, open day deals slot nicely in and resonate with my passion and uniqueness. Copying another dentist and their strategy never works, because you are not them. We are all unique, born with different qualities – you just have to become aware of yours. Like I said, when you do, anything is possible and everything just feels right!

How to find your uniqueness and passion

Why is finding your uniqueness and passion important for a dentist who wants to develop and grow their businesses?

Your competition will not be able to steal your patients

I call him 'Cake Man', but you all know him as Shalin Kapoor, one of the coolest guys in dentistry. Anyway, he used to film himself either making a cake or carving a bar of soap. It was engaging. You could imagine how bloody neat his fillings were if he could make a bar of soap look anatomically perfect. An artist. He opened a dental business with a cracking USP: it was a cartoon-looking joint. Spiderman, famous people. It looked more like Disneyland to me, but it was fun, exact, to the point,

---

Copying another dentist and their strategy never works, because you are not them.

---

clean, welcoming and friendly. Now my point is this: if I set up something similar next door, would I be able to take away his customers? Would that mean Dr Shalin is no longer unique? The answer is of course not. It isn't part of my makeup, my uniqueness or my why, so my cartoon soap carving days would be short lived. Your USP is always deeper than what you are advertising. It is always hidden in the why.

It makes your marketing meaningful and gives it direction

A highly skilled dentist asked me to find her USP after one of my courses. I asked her what excited her about the job. What was it that really motivated her in dentistry? 'The journey, taking the patient through the journey.' Digging a little deeper, I discovered that her father had travelled from India and when she was a child he had regularly talked about this journey. Her upbringing was probably influenced by her father's courage. A lightbulb moment. At that point it dawned on her. There was no point advertising cost-cutting dentistry, or before and after photos, as they weren't part of her core or her why. Her advertising should have been focused on the entire patient journey, relationship building, photos before, during and after treatments showing the bond between the patient and the practice. I think a lot about that dentist. If your marketing and business strategy is in line with your uniqueness and passion, anything is possible and everything makes sense. There will never be another crappy advert that goes out. You will never say to reception, 'Stick an advert out, will you? Make it a good one. Just put out what you think.' It will all just begin to make sense.

It's a guiding star for decision making

Another example was when a dentist phoned me after my Squat Course. He was so excited. Through his excitement he found his lightbulb moment: 'I have worked it out, not just my business but my life makes sense.' His why was the fact that he liked to make people smile. He made me smile. Now that the dentist had direction; he had a reason and direction for his future plans. He became conscious of his uniqueness and got to work on his USP. He had the roots to build something extraordinary and his entire business would be built around making people smile. How totally delightful, how heart-warming.

It makes you a better leader (people will know what you stand for, making you seem more predictable and feel more deliberate)

When your staff and people around you become aware of what your passion is, you can lead them in that direction, and they will know what to expect from you. You won't be unpredictable or offer knee-jerk reactions that leave your team confused. Part of finding your USP is about finding purpose; without that, everyone can be pulling in different directions. You'll feel more in control and you will be seen as such by those you lead.

So, in short, discovering your USP is more than just discovering your marketing strategy and sticking out adverts that make you appear different to your competitors. It is about finding your passion. Getting staff on the bus (or throwing them off – legally!). Staff will have direction. You no longer march in on Monday morning with a new idea or strategy that you picked up from a course that got you all fired up at the weekend, only to crash it out on Tuesday as it wasn't working.

You can make great straplines that mean something

I remember when I started out, designing the strapline for the business really bothered me. I couldn't think of one that motivated or resonated with me. I see those dull straplines everywhere: 'we provide gentle dentistry', 'we treat anxious patients sensitively'. They have no soul. As soon as you are aware of your why, the strapline can be designed to sell your passion. Your uniqueness. It then becomes part of your USP.

You can brand your website so that it resonates with you

When you become aware of your passion and your uniqueness you can then brand your websites accordingly. You can use colours and a language that resonate with you. Everything comes together. You can give your web designer direction rather than them giving you examples of what they think. The control is reversed: you are steering the ship, so let the web designer adjust the sails. Just don't give up full control. You have to tell them the direction you want to go in and they can provide the options. It makes it easier for both of you. It ensures a more harmonious relationship between dentist and marketer.

You can improve your sales skills

If you know what you love, you will be able to sell the treatments you enjoy. If your marketing and USP bring the patients in requesting the treatments you find satisfying, you will be able to improve your conversion rates significantly. I won't lie: I bloody hate root treatments. Get me to try and sell one of those and it would be a train wreck. I can certainly sell a referral for the patient to see someone else though!

Improve conversion rates and you will be richer

As stated previously, money is a dirty word. But if the conversion rates go up, you will earn more money and be able to take more time off with family and loved ones. You will become less stressed and start to enjoy your job.

Please don't ignore the importance of this stage. When it hits you and you finally understand it all, it is like that major lightbulb moment. The dentists I have helped can testify to this. It creates clarity and direction like nothing else. No more walking around in the dark. Discovering your USP is more than just an advert – it can affect your entire working environment. I would go as far as suggesting it can improve your work-life balance.

How to find your USP

We all sell the same bloody thing. Teeth. Yes, we wrap it up in different packages but the public think we all do the same thing. You know what makes a good dentist in the eyes of the public? Neat fillings upper 3 to 3 and, of course, it's pain-free (oh, and cheap as chips).

How bloody sad is that? But it's true! Yes, it could be Invisalign rather than train tracks; it could be microscopes rather than loops for the endodontist, but in the eyes of the public we all do the same thing. So, if you are in search of a USP then it has to be personal. What makes you unique as an individual? Then, when you pinpoint your uniqueness, your entire business has a direction.

Every course I have organised has 20 to 25 delegates. Every time dentists queue up to speak to me at the break, I know what they want, and I see them coming over: 'Can you help me find my USP?' One dentist had 10 to 15 pages of A4 with scribbles. He had attended my course to discover his USP. The dentist was devastated: 'I keep searching and I can't bloody find my USP. Help me!' I turned to the dentist and asked him a few questions. He said his life was filled with searching, seeking to become the best he could be. I said that this was where his uniqueness lay. Hidden. Maybe it was 'the search', maybe he would never find the endgame he was expecting. Maybe his uniqueness was in researching. The constant drive to do his best. Maybe the journey to find the best outcome was in his make up. This was a lightbulb moment for him.

He suddenly realised it wasn't the endgame he was looking for. Yes, he wanted to do the best for his patients, but it was the searching that inspired him. When he realised that his anxiety dropped and the lightbulb went on. USP strategies were now a possibility. 'I will always do my best for you as my patient and will continue to search so you can get that perfect outcome.' To be honest, I would go to a dentist with that attitude. His adverts now had a theme. His strapline would be easy to put together. He was aware of his passion and could sell the treatments he wanted and knew the reasons for his drive. Branding was easy and posting blogs and photographs on his website finally made sense and had a theme. I was doing a lecture at a course a few months later. There was the dentist in the front row. Guess what? He was still searching! But it appeared with less anxiety, as he knew his USP!

Story time. Real life. A dentist I knew was burnt out. Be careful what you wish for: he had a busy practice, complete chaos and big money rolling in, patient after patient. Implants and Invisalign. Stress and GDC investigations. A patient said they hadn't been warned that an implant could fail, and another said they had not understood or signed a consent form. From the outside he was living the dream, with fast cars and a big house! The Instagram dentist! The creators of smiles. They looked like they were riding on a crest of a wave – I bloody love that term.

Anyway, when they spoke to me, they were broken, but I felt I could streamline their business. I could create all sorts of operational systems that would make their life a breeze. Then it happened. The discussion about what they actually wanted in life. What their passion was and, in turn, their uniqueness. Their USP! It turned out that the burnt-out dentist had a passion to learn, a passion to pass that knowledge on to others. That passion was not being fulfilled in their present position. Turns out that dentist went off and started teaching, leaving the nightmare behind. He became a happier person in himself and for those around him.

I always say be careful what you wish for, as your journey to self discovery can lead you down a path you were not expecting! Take me! I got two O levels (rubbish grades) and I became a dentist writing a book! What you set out to do is not necessarily the path you stay on. They also sold the practice for a shed load, leaving all the stress and worries behind.

When I am asked to help dentists find their USP, I always start with a number of questions. For example, I was driving home and a dentist phoned me and was having difficulty working out a USP. I was speaking to a dentist. I asked them what their passion was. I didn't mention dentistry. They answered with such energy: 'I just love the thank you at the end of treatment; I love being appreciated. I love the end of treatment when they are smiling, and I value the trust they are putting in me.' No mention of doing neat fillings, doing a good job. Or crap like 'gentle dentistry', 'quality care with quality equipment'. So a true USP, in my opinion, has nothing to do with dentistry. It is a part of you, a part of your soul. Your why. It's why you put up with a highly regulated profession with nothing to look forward to but a lifetime in a job with the highest drug, alcohol and suicide rate of all the medical professions. This lovely dentist valued being trusted. That was not just dentistry. That went far beyond the highspeed drill. It went somewhere deeper. This particular dentist wanted to treat children and the elderly. I would take my children to a dentist who had a USP dedicated to the trust they want to build with their patients and their children.

Exercise

Back to discovering your why; find your uniqueness and passion, and then we can choose the vehicle to get that message out in the form of your USP. But remember that to get your USP you need to go through a journey.

Firstly, you have to establish your uniqueness, then your unique selling point is the vehicle you use to reveal it to the world! When you become aware of your unique qualities, no one can be the same. No one can copy you; no one can race you to the bottom.

You will have why you do what you do with such enthusiasm in a profession that has so much stress, anxiety, depression and divorce. You will be aware of why you jump out of bed and put up with Mrs Smith. You'll remember how you can find joy in a job that is rated as one of the most stressful professions known to man. (Well, it was. Apparently, it is a marriage therapist now! They're probably dealing with too many dentists!)

Back to the process!

Stage 1: What's your passion?

There are 5 passions. Concentrate and discover which one resonates with you.

1. **To feel.** This relates to the importance you place on *how you feel* about treating a patient. How you feel about doing a good job. Does this feeling drive you to produce that masterpiece of a filling? When you have done an amazing job, the actual satisfaction comes from taking pride in the outcome. The feeling of self-satisfaction is higher than the positive validation you get from a patient when they like your work: 'I did a good job' rather than 'I am thrilled with the job you did for me.' Which one floats your boat? Which one really hits home and gives you that positive vibe?

2. **To bond.** Are you addicted to the *patient relationship*? The journey. Do you value the patient staying with you for a lifetime and building deep and meaningful patient-

dentist relationships? Do you feel alive when they bring their entire family to the surgery, as they have developed a lasting trust with you? Do you hold this as the pinnacle of your success? Do you enjoy documenting or photographing different stages of the treatment? For me, I like to straighten their teeth and send them upstairs for routine dentistry going forward, so I realised this clearly wasn't a passion of mine!

3. **To defend.** It is the overwhelming power to defend your patch. Will you stop at nothing to *prevent the competition* from setting up next door? It can also relate to the way one might have an overwhelming passion to defend another, sticking up for them, doing the right thing, being a good person. I remember on many occasions I would ethically (somewhat morally questionable) prevent or try to resist dentists setting up on my patch. I would buy property (well, I would pull out at the last minute) driving up the price of a building, complain about planning applications – the list goes on. I am not proud of myself for this, but I recognised early on in my life that this passion resonates with me acutely. I will also support and stand by others who are loyal to me.

4. **To acquire.** Do you have a *passion to build*, to have more money or fast cars? Do you want to build more and more dental practices? This passion can lead to much misery, so be aware of it and make sure it is balanced. It could mean anything from having a good pay packet at the end of the month to having 25 sports cars sitting outside your house.

There is nothing wrong with this passion. This passion resonates strongly with me, coupled with the passion to defend. Many dentists have a passion to acquire and they post their cars and houses on social media. There will be many congratulatory comments. Mark my words – another dentist with a passion to acquire will be seething, having private thoughts about punching you in the throat. The dentists with a passion to feel and to bond will think you are bloody mad to spend so much money on a car, but they will still appreciate the beauty of how it looks. For me, I have never understood why someone would buy a £200,000 car and sit it on a driveway of a rubbish house, but that is just me.

5. **To learn.** Did you finish your dental degree and *keep learning*? Do you have degrees and more degrees after your name? Do you want to go on endless dental courses? Do you like researching different treatments and options for your patients? Do you get inspired by others that know more? Do you want to keep expanding your mind? I always think about this passion. I certainly did not want to study after university. Nearly had my first nervous breakdown during my finals. I swore to myself never again. I see some dentists going on course after course. I love marketing and advertising. I love analysing the human psyche and how we operate. But this is a hobby and I do not consider it learning in the sense of this passion. I respect others who have this passion and drive. This group will help push our profession further. To the limits. They find new and better ways to do things.

Now we know the five passions, we will have one that stands out from the rest. You may have a mixture of a few but there is always one that hits home. The question I then get asked is how I adapt it to find my USP. When you know which passion drives you, you are more than halfway there. Don't get me wrong, there are a host of self-reflective analyses that can be carried out to establish why a particular passion resonates with you. Mine was from the days of boarding school and middle child stuff, but it really isn't necessary to delve that deeply into a journey of self-discovery unless it interests you.

You are aware of your passion now, so you have to turn it into a USP, showing the world what your passion is. You have to make sure that anything you put out to the public is in line with your passion. The marketing message can push the boundaries of your passion, though. So a dentist with a passion to learn can in fact advertise cost-cutting open days, but not on a regular basis, as it will become an irritant. However, that cost-cutting open day would suit the dentist with a passion to acquire and to defend. Beat the competition. I have a rolling open day advert and love it!

However, there is one point that needs to hit home: running a business requires an element of ruthlessness. Business is business. Though it doesn't always have to be about stepping on necks, crushing the competition, blasting them out of the water, torpedoing their marketing strategy. Even for the dentists with a passion to defend. I remember when I was going to set up a squat practice next to Mitesh Badiani in Ashburton. Instead of blasting me out of the water, he asked me to meet up and go for a drink. I remember thinking he wasn't being nice and welcoming me to the neighbourhood.

On the contrary, I thought he was asking me out for a drink to let me know he had zero fear and he actually didn't give a damn about my possible effect on his business if I set up next door to him. I didn't set up in his street for those very reasons. 15 years on we are friends and it turns out he was just being nice. I was overthinking and my passion to defend was being projected onto him. His passion was to bond. How wrong can we be?

Use your passion as a benchmark – a cornerstone – and you will never go too far off the beaten track.

Stage 2: What's your USP?

What do you do now you know your passion? How do you translate it into a USP?

1. Branding – websites and logos
2. Strapline
3. Marketing and advertising
4. Analysing your competition

Step 1: Branding

There are some big players designing websites within the dental profession. I do think dentists, including me, are a funny lot. Very fickle. If we sniff a bad service, it goes around like wildfire. So, if you can survive in the dental business world, you have my respect for sure.

Digimax is one of those businesses. Branding and web designs. Shaz Memon is a big character in the dental world. He definitely has a passion to defend. It is safe to say Digimax is one of the leading go-to firms for web designs. I am no graphic designer but when you see one of his websites – the page just looks nice, it just works. Still trying to work out why!? I am sure that dentists ring him up and say, 'I don't know what I want, but sort me a nice logo and branding and build me a nice website that looks all cool and gets me loads of patients.' What a nightmare that must be. You are putting all the onus on him to create what should be coming from you.

Another web designer I respect is Shehbaz Ashraf. The new kid on the block. His websites also have a touch of genius. They are two different designers, and poles apart, but I recommend both of them when asked. It isn't about getting a cheap job. It is about having that artistic flare. Having that end result that is in line with your passion and ultimate USP! Remember your website and USP are the roots of your STFD business model. The gateway to your business! It's crucial you nail this.

Next time you ring up a web designer, give them a little more to build on. Did you know that each passion has an associated colour!? It's easy to find. Use Google.

To defend – black (protection), red (strength)

To learn – blue (learn), red, orange, yellow (increased knowledge)

To acquire – green (build & money)

To bond – yellow (friendship)

To feel – red (anger/frustration), yellow (fear), indigo (compassion), violet (love)

I am not saying you have to stick to the rules, but it gives you a start. Work out your passion, find the colour, it may work for you, but it may not. It just gives you an idea. It gives you some ingredients for firms like Idesign Dental (Shehbaz) and Digimax (Shaz) to start working on your project. Logos are the same. I would brief a designer on my passion and my colours and let them go to work. I am a stingy sod, so I used 99designs to create my logos www.99designs.co.uk

Step 2: Strapline

My strapline is: 'To be informed and to have the choice.' It may seem extremely bland and boring. To me, it has always been the cornerstone of all the businesses I have built (not just dentistry). I believe that everyone deserves and has a right to all the information before having to make a decision. My passion to defend and to bond is associated with this strapline.

Other straplines I have found associated with dental practices with the following apparent passions:

To learn
'Quality is the result of intelligent effort.'

To defend
'We are not your general dentist, we are your personal dentist.'

To feel
'A beautiful smile is your passport to love.'

To bond
'We work hard to make sure you smile more.'

To acquire
'Bright, beautiful and straight teeth for less.'

I am not saying any of these are perfect. In fact, I sense you are sitting there saying how crap some of them are, but that is OK. You are not supposed to copy these. You need to find your own that resonates with you. Think about your passion and brainstorm how that plays out in the type of practice you run.

Step 3: Marketing & Advertising

Anyone who knows me knows this is what I love, finding that approach, that angle that will resonate with not only my clients but myself as well. This is the most powerful part of the process and the most crucial. You are presenting your offering to the world. Whatever your passion, you need to be responsible for your business and make sure the patients choose you and not the dentist up the road. Marketing and advertising are the vehicle you use to shout more loudly and clearly than the competition. We can now call it your USP: your unique selling point!

Find your passion and then relate it to your marketing strategy.

A Passion to Learn

Present your case. Show your intelligence. Start blogging with the *Resource Pack: Task 4*. There you'll find a video demonstrating how to SEO a blog on a WordPress website. You could also produce articles in the local paper. If you have dedicated your life to study, you must show that. Do not put out open day deals that simply will not resonate with you.

It is OK to do this occasionally, just do not let it be your cornerstone. Work out ways to spread the word about your training and experience. I once saw an advert by a specialist who claimed they were far better trained than the local dentists with a special interest. Whilst this was an approach, it wasn't the approach I would recommend. Never put anyone down to make yourself look better. If this is you, always talk about yourself rather than compare your skills to others.

A Passion to Defend

This is quite an aggressive form of marketing. It has a similar theme to acquire, but it is more aggressive. If this is you, create content around what you're great at – the dental awards should be splashed over your website. This is what ticks all the dentists off who have a passion to learn: they hate the awards. They feel it is misleading the public. Oh, get stuffed. They plaster over their websites, they lecture this and lecture that. That is equally misleading! Remember, do not compare yourself. Look at what others are advertising and create adverts that are clearly better. Better photography, better prices, better content. You are in it to win. You are there to do better and defend what is yours. There is absolutely nothing wrong with this type of marketing. Just remain professional and do not put anyone down. Look at Avis car hire: 'We are the second biggest car hire firm, so we try harder.' How amazingly clever is that!

A Passion to Feel

These dentists love their stuff! Their fillings are perfect. They post their implant placements – no patients in the photo, just their beautiful teeth carved to perfection. They may carve a tooth out of plasticine or make a cake that looks anatomically perfect. They are usually extremely artistic and their photography is perfect. Their websites are filled with perfect photos and perfect teeth. I think this is a very powerful form of advertising as it makes them look like perfectionists. If they can make a tooth out of a bit of clay, I bet they can carve a great filling and really care about the outcome. If this is you, then get those photos out there. If you have a passion to bond, throw in a few face shots as well. It is always good to bring your work to life!

A Passion to Bond

The journey. This group loves the journey that they go on with a patient. I lack a bit of this. I would prefer in and out, a great outcome and job done, but this group of dentists want to nurture the relationship. They build long-term patients with great customer service. The marketing should reflect this drive. If this is you, post photos about the patient's journey, shaking hands, showing photos of the different stages, for example. Have testimonials stating how long the patient has been with you and why. Let the patients speak your words, your sentiments, your passion. This is a very powerful passion to embrace. It is what most human beings yearn for and miss when it is absent.

A Passion to Acquire

This group just loves to build. This group is criticised, as colleagues think it is the race to the bottom or they are changing dentistry into a commodity. I think that is crap. There is only a race to the bottom if someone else joins in. If you find yourself not in this group and trying to compete – don't! This group is highly skilled and extremely aggressive. They will also not lose this game. They will carry on cutting costs until you are both on your knees. They will then find other ways to cut further. If this is you, post about price discounts, costs of treatment, patient plans, interest-free credit. Post about how many associates you have and how you offer all different types of treatments. Post all the buildings you work from. Who cares? Post everything about the number! It's all about the number.

Step 4: Analyse your competition

When you are selling yourself to the world you now have an ingredient and an action and a plan! It is only responsible to look around. Does anyone else's USP look like yours? You can have two USPs that look similar in the same town. Why? Because they come from two different people with two different unique qualities.

You just have to see what's on offer by others and how it is being presented. When I hear dentists say ignore what everyone else is doing and just concentrate on your own game… what a bucket of pish. Of course, don't be led by others but be guided in your offerings – there is nothing wrong with switching your direction slightly. Just make sure you keep your passion and uniqueness firmly at the roots of all your decisions and make sure you do better than your competitors!

How do I research competitors?

1. Give them a call to see how good their reception staff are. Doesn't matter how fancy their website is or how perfectly placed their USP is, if their staff can't answer the phone,

then game on. As stated, 95% of all our mystery shops to dental practices failed last year. The Mystery Shop form is in the *Resource Pack: Task 5*. This will give you an idea of the basic questions any business should be getting right! Reception wages are the lowest paid yet they should be one of the highest priorities to get right. I have never quite understood why we pay them peanuts. Saying that, it is the same with nurses! Calculate how much you can lose when they aren't there! Then it will give you an indication of their importance.

2. Have a chat in the local coffee shop. Ask the waitress if there is a decent dentist in town. Pick the coffee shop that has the counter and tables in the same room. Gossip is a wonderful thing. The workers live to tell all. They will stand at the counter and give you the rundown of all the local dentists.

3. Ask the local estate agents. I found this was always a great way to find out about the dentists in the area. I always made it my priority to visit the estate agents. They are the ones recommending local businesses to new residents.

4. Finally, use all the free stuff on the internet. See how many organic patients visit their site a month, look at their prices. Look at the colours, branding and overall feel. The following sites are free and will tell you an awful lot about the enemy. Oops, did I say enemy?

www.spyfoo.com
www.neilpatel.com

So, there you have it. Your uniqueness – your USP – and how to find it/discover it through your passion. Then, how you present it to the world around you. When you release a post, an advert, employ a member of staff, ask yourself if it all falls in line with your passion. It won't always be the case. You won't always make the right decisions. Remember there are others in the business that each have their own passion and uniqueness and will bring a different ingredient to your pot. Maybe part of your uniqueness includes the passion to bond, to accept the advice and help of others. Maybe it isn't and you just ignore the member of staff, as you know better. We all make mistakes and no one is perfect. I am far from it!

Client Story: A Passion to Bond

In 2019, I worked with a dentist who was close to burning out. He hated the job, had miserable patients and miserable staff he worked with. Well, that was what he was feeling. He and his partner were about to have a baby, so stress levels were really high. Work was an uphill struggle and he could never fully engage in treatments he was providing or the staff he was working with. This dentist broke down on the phone to me. The overall feeling was that he felt he was treading water. Not getting anywhere and the stress of the newborn, he realised he had to sort himself out and fast. The dentistry he was doing was not inspiring. He felt deflated by life in general, but work was the main focus of his misery.

I started by discussing the five passions, as I wanted to discover what resonated with him. It turned out to be the journey. He loved the bond that was created between him and the patient during the treatment. He loved how the patients came back with their friends and family to have treatment, enjoying the relationships that he built with his patients. He also had great satisfaction when he received Christmas presents from grateful patients.

When I highlighted the passion to bond it became more conscious – it dawned on him the mini-corporate was all about the number. One in one out. There was little focus on patient retention. Testimonials were rarely asked for and staff were not geared up to provide a five-star service. It was a basic drill and fill business.

Don't get me wrong, that would suit many dentists. Just not my client. When he became aware of the dentistry he wanted to do it made the reasons for his sadness clear; it was the lightbulb moment. You cannot go against your passion. It will create internal struggles and eventually you will burn out.

So, in going against the grain, in pushing back against his passions, it made him miserable.

My job was done. Eighteen months later that very dentist opened a practice of his own. My oh my, what a place it was; he spent a fortune. I have the passion to acquire so I would have saved and not spent the level of budget, but to see the opening day, to see that dentist smile, certainly resonated with me. The passion to bond and feel shone through. I didn't pay the bills so I allowed myself to feel that sense of pride. Only when that dentist became aware of his passion did his career take a different direction. One of total job satisfaction. To be fair, I still would have drawn the line at an £8k reception desk, but three years later they have no regrets: 'It is what my patients first see; it's how they will first judge me; it is what

I build relationships upon.' If you are reading this book, you know who you are and I have the utmost respect for you my friend.

Martina Hodgson is an extremely successful businessperson, a female dentist ready to take on the fight. Equal opportunities for women. This is a fight I fully support. If you think you are better because you are male that makes you a special type of bellend.

Martina is about to build a bloody massive business. (By the time this book is released the practice will have been built and it will have been an astonishing success.) When I look at her business the unique selling point appears to me to be attention to detail. An inclusive development where the entire team is part of the journey. There is no cost spared when it comes to developing the operational side of the business and making the team within a happy crew. What an amazing place to have your teeth done!

Do you see what I am getting at? If your attention to detail is spot on, if you can make a cake that looks identical to the teeth you are drilling, your work must also be equally perfect. No person with that level of care and attention to detail would be a bad dentist. It is about the subconscious message we are putting out to our potential client base. 'If you have your teeth done by me, you will see I will treat you like I treat my family, my staff, my sculptures. I will strive to be the best I can be for you.' What a powerful message. And the beauty of it? It is free! It costs nothing to display your greatness to the world. You just have to be aware of what you are doing. Then exploit it!

The difference between successful dentists and ones who are struggling is down to being aware of their passion and uniqueness. Everything they do seems to be hung on this – adverts, surgery design, staff relationships – and in doing so they seem to enjoy their job and be a total success.

Success is not always the bank balance or size of your wallet or type of house or car! (Remember that it can be for some and that is OK.)

Find your uniqueness; make sure your drive is in line with this passion and success will follow, and that success can be in many forms. Did you know that is why bonuses at work never last? It always ticks staff off in the end because staff haven't had the chance to let you know what they want. If Kim on the desk has a rich husband who provides for her, why would she be driven by money? Why would Lauren want time off when she is building a house and would appreciate financial support to help with purchasing furniture? So, if you want to get everyone on your bus – ship, whatever – find out what is important to the ones you want to get onboard with your vision.

Summary

Hopefully uniqueness, USP and passion are all now a little clearer, as is how they all slot into the business of dentistry. I don't know why some people are better at locating it within themselves than others. It took me 20 years of therapy to fully appreciate my uniqueness, but it was always there. I always used my passion and uniqueness to build all the businesses I developed. It was just at a more subconscious level. I do know it takes a lot of soul searching and it can be quite painful to look inwardly at oneself. To question why you feel and behave in a certain way. Other than narcissists, I think anyone can do this. It just takes time. Time is all we have. Time and a great deal of courage.

CHAPTER 6

OPERATIONAL

My story

Before thinking about the operational branch of the tree, I would look at others and I would see them post about 'systems in place'. I remember thinking they must be great businesspeople. Why? Cause I didn't even know what an operational system was, never mind having any in place. The systems were clearly very effective, as they oiled the business and enabled their businesses to work seamlessly. It allowed the owner to work on the business rather than in it. Hate that saying. On it not in it. I don't know why it gets me so irritated. We all work in a business, but it has become a buzz sentence in dentistry.

Before the days of any type of organisation, my business was almost a fluke. Yes, I could build a business: *Field of Dreams* starring Kevin Costner, 'If you build it, they will come', that was me. But after they came (the patients), I would have no bloody clue how to organise anything. Get the patient in, get the patient in the chair, collect the dollar, job done – it ain't rocket science. And it did work. I built a super squat this way. Eight surgeries in three years. It was not only one of the fastest growing squat practices but also one of the biggest in Devon. However, I say this: thank goodness IDH took it off my hands. It was organised bloody chaos.

I was stressed out, in therapy once a week, and I was holding on too tightly without the opportunity to take a bird's eye view of the business. Staff were not accountable. Yes, accountability is the key to a business. That is what will make it flourish. If staff think you are watching them, if staff think they are under the spotlight, they will work harder. I had none of this. I literally went from one disorganised business problem to another. Patients who were willing to spend £48k on full arch reconstructions were not contacted, ClinChecks were forgotten about, lab work would get lost. It was a bloody shambles. I remember, back in the day, I had no clue about how to run a business. I wish I could go back to that young fella who had a massive ego, a passion to defend and acquire, and talk to him. But I have to accept I am 52 years old now and, if it wasn't for all the screw ups I made, I wouldn't be here writing a book, showing you how easy all this stuff is.

When I designed an operating system, I managed to relax a little and catch my breath. Having control does not make you a control freak.

What makes you a good businessperson? I was able to spot where the holes in my bucket were. I could patch the holes before I filled it with more water. I stopped bleeding new patients. Basically, my gross turnover shot up and expenses went down. How did I feel? Fan-bloody-tastic.

What's this step all about?

This trunk of the tree – this branch – is all about having a system that gives you not only a bird's eye view of your business, but it allows you to plot the whole patient journey from start to finish. You can monitor where the baton is dropped, where the patient is lost and where money is being left on the table. Viewing the journey is an incredible tool.

I had a patient last week. Yes, I still carry out clinical dentistry. They wanted full arch bridges. Upper and lower. Estimated cost £42,000. I always ask patients what brings them to my door. What made them book in with me? In this case, the only reason was that I was the only person that responded to their enquiry. They had contacted eight other businesses across Devon and Cornwall. Eight! How staggering! How very sad that eight practice owners go to bed at night unaware of their staff and their response to high-end treatment enquiries. But it doesn't stop there. The reputation of the business is at stake: a hole in the bucket, a break in the chain. Mend the break, mend the bucket, then you can start filling the bucket with more water. For goodness' sake, do not fill the broken bucket with more water to solve the issue. Get a good operational system in place and you can spot where the issues are. Blindly run your business and you will blindly spend your budget. I cannot stress this enough – if you do not take care of the patient, they will not take care of you. The patients want to be respected, they want to be contacted in response to their enquiry, they want to be kept up to date with their journey.

I bought a building on the main street for £300k and recently sold it to Portman for millions including the building, cash held and goodwill. I can safely say that the success of the practice was down to the fact that I had a good operational system. I learned the hard way with an earlier business, by working without having the right systems in place.

For an earlier business, my first squat practice, I bought the building in a good location in Devon for £70k and grew it over a three-year period. It was a private practice with eight surgeries (a super squat). I then sold it to IDH (my dentist), but it half killed me because I didn't have any operational systems in place. Without any operation systems, I bled patients, bled staff, put money into marketing that didn't bring ROI. With a lack of analysis and accountability it felt like it was a shambles. I was working long hours, exhausted. I had grown a bigger bucket without taking time to work out where the holes were that needed plugging. With the other business to follow, they were beautiful well-oiled machines. They were also easier to sell and I could command a higher price because the buyer could see that everything was transparent and well organised.

Before I sold my last business, when I steered the ship, one of my competitors always dropped the baton. He was probably one of the best clinical surgeons in the area, an absolute natural. I always knew patients would end up in my chair, though. After seeing the surgeon, they wouldn't get that call back, that follow up appointment or patient care they expected. The treatment estimates would be forgotten and not sent out as promised. The operational arm of the business was poor.

Jas Gill – He is a well-known dentist who has established himself on the lecturing circuit. His business seems to be one big operational system. He seems to have checks on the checks that check the hundreds of systems in place. Nothing goes missing in his business, patients do not get missed. This is how you become a big Invisalign provider in a poor area. His team never drop the baton.

On the other side of the coin, another local competitor was much better qualified than I. They had carried out so many more hours of CPD and extra qualifications and honed their skills. They had built a business that had so much potential but, to be brutally honest, I owe them. I owe them a massive drink because of their sloppy systems; because of the poor operational branch of the STFD business model, I was able to clean up in my area. That was to the tune of millions of pounds. How brilliant it was for me, how devastating for them. One day they may read this book. One day I will remind them that I tried; I once called them to say their reception team were appalling and one of their team was so rude it was costing them dearly. Maybe they will listen, maybe they won't care.

What if I could show you a system that allows you to have a bird's eye view of your business? What if I could make every staff member accountable? What if I could give you an operational system that will give you total control? What if I told you it was free? We dentists love a freebie!

If you get your operational branch of the tree sorted, if you create a little order in your business, I promise you your life will be much easier. You will have a sense of control. Staff will even thank you for it. Trust me: you have come this far and you have stuck with me, so wait for this system; you only need one in place and it is not only genius but it is free too!

Why is it particularly important for dentists wanting to grow?

It allows the growth to occur more smoothly. An operational system gives you a bird's eye view of the business which makes everything well oiled. It allows a control from the top down. It sets up accountability and control, from establishing advert ROI, through to reception, from associate conversion rates to ensuring the baton is not dropped and patients are not forgotten. How cool is that? A total system in one place!

It's the ultimate funnel system

We all love talking about funnels! The system is the ultimate funnel! All enquiries go into one area. It then splits the low-ticket enquiries (NHS or general dentistry) and the high-ticket enquiries (cosmetic dentistry – orthodontics, veneers and implants). I am not saying the NHS is less important (that is a different debate for a different day!) but the splitting of the treatment enquiries allows the reception team to apportion the new patients accordingly. This enables the right patient to go to the right dentist at the right time, improving productivity!

Advert ROI

We all love the number. We all love to know if our investment is working. The operational system enables you to see if that advert has brought the patients to your door. It will show you which adverts you need to concentrate more on and which ones you need to drop. It can save you thousands in lost revenue whilst improving your turnover significantly.

Reception team accountability

We blame marketers for rubbish leads when our receptionists either don't answer the phone or, when they do, are rude and obnoxious. We are almost at the level of a GP surgery. When I rock up to my doctors' the receptionists always ask me what my problem is. The waiting room is packed. Every time, I want to blurt out that I have a massive genital rash that I seem to be passing on to everyone I sit near. But I haven't found the courage. Nosey old boot – the reasons I want to see my GP are private and nothing to do with the miserable receptionist staring back at me. Point being – if this was a private service I would seek out a competitor despite how much I respect and like the GP herself.

Here is a screenshot of one of my mystery shops my team carried out last year.

On answering the phone?	More than 5 rings
Request for your name?	No
Asked where you heard of the business?	No
Asked you any questions?	No
Built any rapport?	No
Knew the prices of treatment?	No
Manner?	Not pleasant
Asked you to book an appointment (Closed)	No
Experience?	Poor
Further comments	Phone took 3 mins to be answered
	Asked the price of whitening. Was told to 'hang on'. Heard her in the background asking for price of whitening. She then say to colleague, "I don't know why they can't look on the f&@king website".
	Came back on the phone to me and said we don't know, you'll have to call back. Then hung up.
Would you book an appointment?	No

The receptionist thought they were on mute and said to her colleague that if I want to know the price of whitening I should 'look on the damn website'. We will cover the customer and people branch later in the book, but the operational system enables us to see which receptionist is crap! In turn, it reduces the possibility of losing a patient to the competition. If a new patient comes through the door the reception team need to make sure they get to see you before making the decision not to come back!

Dental associate accountability

We all know associates will never worry about the business as much as the owner (that isn't always the case, but it is usually), and naturally so! Why should they? This system will enable you to see which associates are converting the treatments and which ones are draining the new patient numbers. It will also help when confronted by the angry associate asking why they aren't getting all the new patients when compared with the other dentists in the building – you will have the numbers! When the associates become accountable and you can demonstrate that you can analyse the new patients, the associates will step up their game. The turnover will also go up.

The baton will never get dropped

The system will allow you to give a constant reminder to the reception team to take deposits and ensure the patients are booked in and not forgotten.

Less stressful life

The key thing is that you know you are no longer losing patients and money. It is soul destroying to hear a patient who wanted a £30k treatment plan has been forgotten, and they no longer want to visit you because of the poor customer care. The soul-destroying element is that you know that if you ran a tighter ship, you could have and should have prevented that loss. It feels like such a waste when you have the opportunity to be better. Staff will appreciate the order and structure whilst the improvement in customer care will make everybody's life easier.

When you're in control and you know what's going on in your business there are no knee-jerk reactions, no nasty surprises and less energy is spent putting out fires.

Accountability

Why is accountability so crucial? Because it promotes a self-disciplined approach to work: 'If I do this, I am being watched.' I don't mean the creepy boss who stands behind the receptionist massaging their shoulders. By the way, if you are a boss and you massage the receptionist's shoulders, please don't do that. It is not only illegal, but it also makes you extremely creepy, and they are squirming because of you. Back to my operational system – I don't mean these creeps who are staring at every staff member's move. I mean a system that allows everybody to see everybody. It isn't a negative influence; it is a positive 'let's grow together' approach. Organised and free of chaos. Don't get me wrong, I have worked with many dentists who feel they are the only ones that need to see. They are the only ones who require that total control. A number of these dentists are incredibly successful, but they are stressed out and knackered, having clocked up a couple of divorces and kids they don't see much. We are all accountable for the work we do. We are our own critics. And when there is a risk, your colleagues can see your gains and losses, then you step up and try harder. It is human nature.

It's a joint responsibility. Where there is a joint responsibility, customer care is second to none.

It improves your strategic decision making

To summarise, when you are able to analyse a business, you are able to evaluate how needs changed, what you can do better and what needs to remain unchanged. It also shows you which receptionist is lazy and incapable of converting a patient from enquiry to booking. You can then offer the right training or which door to leave by. It also provides vital information, for example how many consultations a dentist is provided without converting to treatment and which dentists might need some extra training or support. And the beauty of it? They can bloody see it all as well. Everyone is accountable because everyone can see it for themselves. It is one hell of a motivator. **It keeps clients happy, ensures you are not losing sales through the cracks** and, I tell you what, it not only keeps staff happy but the patients as well! They will be contacted in a timely fashion; they won't be forgotten, so they will be made to feel special. If I was to sum it all up in one sentence: you won't drop the baton ever again.

Have you ever tried to expand and develop a business without control? I bloody have. The stress just keeps piling on. More chaos, more staff, more chaos, more stress, more staff! There will be more money over the desk but you will notice that it doesn't equate to more cash in the bank (profit). I remember those days when I would look at the monthly takings and I was overwhelmed with my apparent success, only to go to the bank and see I had made a loss! A bloody loss. How did that happen? I used to phone my dad, a retired dentist, for reassurance. The dental profession is an odd one. One minute I was planning which Ferrari I was going to buy, the next worrying I couldn't keep the wolves from the door; the fear of losing my house became overwhelming, only to find me back down to the sports car showroom the following month. It is an oddity – it is a strange common trait in our business. Many clients suffer in this way, the way I did, riding on the crest of a wave one minute to the depths of hell the next. So, for you to have a more stable financial business – the business needs accountability and analysis. It gives you the capability to view how everyone works and where the baton is being dropped! If staff push back and refuse to embrace your new ideas, go and speak to Phil Clark from Peninsula. Sometimes, if you are getting pushback from staff about the operational system you want to introduce, it might not be about the operating system but about that particular member of staff being frightened of change. Just remember, we all have different passions that make us unique. Always be kind and understand that everyone is different, but if they are still reluctant to change after all of that – then you can kick them off the bloody bus.

Client Story: A Passion to Acquire

What was happening and what was going wrong?

I spoke to a dear friend and client in early 2021. He is loaded, having had a number of businesses all over Birmingham. Each business had a couple of hundred thousand pounds in credit in the bank, so he was sitting nicely. A passion to acquire! He was building and buying! Literally taking over the world. He said money meant little to him. I felt like saying 'That's because you have so bloody much of it.' Anyway, he was in desperate need of two things: a holiday and control of his businesses. He was growing too fast and too quickly. No word of a lie, he was receiving 200 enquiries per week per business. A website with 6k visitors a month. He also refused to turn off any advertising in the fear that this chaos (albeit a good chaos) would stop and all the leads would dry up. By the way, there is a happy place between a chaotic shed load of enquiries and zero leads. There is a middle ground whereby the leads can be nurtured and not forgotten, but my friend and client was working in an environment of chaos. A victim of his own success, he was desperate to know if his business was in a chaotic mess or he had fluked it and it was a fine well-oiled machine.

What was the result of this chaos? We will never know the scale of lost income. I carried out a mystery shop for each of his businesses – ten in total (another three more in the pipeline). They all failed. One receptionist said I shouldn't have veneers as they damaged teeth. One said I should go back to the website to find their prices. 'I have already looked on the website, for goodness sake; that's how I know the phone number.' Another didn't answer the phone. Another was rude and obnoxious. Showing the owner the results of the mystery shop is always an enlightening session. Suddenly they realise the impact of chaos and how it affects their business. Remember, 190 mystery shops and 188 failed. That is billions of lost revenue. That is your kids' education, a house or a dream car.

Don't get me wrong, having the phone ring and patients wanting to book in is half the battle. But only half. The other half has to be about organisation and operational systems. Sometimes having so many leads and enquiries is more stressful when the system isn't oiled than having a few leads that are nurtured and bear fruit! The gain is far sweeter than the loss felt when leads are missed, the baton is dropped. Seeing money lost has far more impact. It used to destroy me when a patient was forgotten. Seeing what could have been is a horrible feeling. And when patients are treated well, they become loyal – and what does loyalty mean in the dental world? A patient that will be with you a lifetime. One that brings their friends, their family, their loved ones. Something far more financially beneficial than an implant or a set of Invisalign braces to a patient that will leave you after the work is complete.

If I was going to scale it from 1 to 10, with 1 being awful and 10 being perfection, the business had 10/10 potential but 1/10 for fulfilling their potential. Wasted talent. When I say how bad it was… I think that out of all the businesses the group owned, one well-run practice could have earnt the same profit with a fraction of the stress. But the passion to acquire was dominating his decision making. Just don't forget to incorporate the operational systems to ensure your growth and subsequent increase in stress is all worth it.

So, where did we start?

I remember when I started my journey towards emotional well-being. I would sit in front of my therapist and almost demand a solution to a problem I was experiencing. If Grace couldn't offer me a quick solution, I wanted to know the steps towards making the issue go away. The response was always the same. The hardest bit is to recognise there is an issue and a change is needed. That positive confirmation, that conscious promise to yourself, is always the hardest part of any change. The business of dentistry is just the same. Admitting your operational processes are lacking, that patients are not well processed and that there is no accountability for staff carrying out these processes is painful, but it is not about failure! Most businesses float around with zero organisation. Some just fluke it. You think the 15-year-old who made billions out of a software they invented, in between masturbating and picking spots, had any operational processes? No! So, it doesn't mean success or failure. It is about making your life easier, having a happier team and earning more money.

However, if you embrace the idea, admitting to yourself that life could be a little easier and that you want to spend more time doing the actual dental treatment you enjoy, this system will work for you. So, the first step is admitting you could do with a little help, a little support and a little bit of organisation. The next step is a massive amount of courage, as change is a bitch – and you will always get pushback from staff. There is always one! We can cover that in later chapters.

So, what did we do?

We introduced the operational system I have created with Donna Hewitt into his businesses. It allowed him to have a bird's eye view of all their practices at the touch of a button.

The operational system that we created captured patients' details and monitored the entire journey all the way through to treatment completion. It enabled my client to analyse his staff properly for the first time, but it actually went one step further. It allowed staff to analyse each other. Total and 100% accountability. It demonstrated where the chain was broken and where he was bleeding patients. Like I said, if there are holes in a bucket, there is no point filling it with more water. There's no point increasing a marketing budget or getting staff training if the break is elsewhere.

What was the result?

When his ten practices embraced the operational system, it enabled him to work on other parts of the business that made everything more efficient. He was no longer working in a chaotic environment. He could make better business decisions because he knew where those holes in his bucket were. Assessment, diagnosis and plan of action! And most importantly he was no longer leaving thousands of pounds on the table every month.

When he embraced this operating system, he managed to get that bird's eye view of everything. Small changes happened. Small changes that created massive increases to profit. They noticed one member of the reception team was unproductive, they never contacted the patients, their conversion from website enquiry to booking was close to 2%. There was an associate who moaned about not having enough new patients. It was discovered they were provided with the most new patients in the attempt to prop up gaps in their appointment book. Gaps were due to their poor conversion skills. Giving them all the new patients was like throwing more water in the broken bucket!

When the issues became clear, they stepped up training. This is not an American film! It doesn't always end well! They lost both members of staff, but their replacements were far more productive. The new associate was sharp, conversion skills were excellent, and the new receptionist was on the ball. Patients were contacted. Sometimes it is out with the old and in with the new, and sometimes it is just guidance and training, but you need to know where attention is needed, where you can direct your energy rather than blindly building a business. Not being able to see or analyse and a lack of accountability are killers for any modern business. Unfortunately, it is a killer not just in the dental profession.

He was able to take more time off knowing that his personal income was not propping up the business. He was happier and less stressed. His business became a highly efficient machine and his gross turnover doubled. It doesn't have to take a divorce or a stress-related illness to give you the wake-up call – try my operational system now! So, I think it's time to introduce you to my operational system. I call it the RoboReception LeadTracker. It is the funnel! The ultimate operational system.

Check out what other dentists say about the RoboReception LeadTracker!

Ahmad Abouserwel
The system has saved us a lot of time and brought us an average of 10 leads per week.

Carol Somerville Roberts
*It's made such a difference to the number of enquiries we get, especially as the system is designed to weed out late night, slightly drunk internet surfers. Thank you **Grant McAree** and the brilliant **Donna Hewitt**!*

Rik Trivedi
We have also started using this and so far we are getting very good results and impressed!!

Martin Kelly
Love it, never miss a lead!

Mohsin Uddin
*My emails are full of leads, thank God. Wish **Grant McAree** would turn up and see these consults.*

Ahmed Giaziri
We've had our number of enquiries double since using it – it's a fantastic lead catcher and CRM in one.

Israr Razaq
We've had some great results and it delivers the results Grant promised me!

Brad Thornton

I used to have another system and I've switched to RoboReception. The change was seamless. It has saved me a chunk of money and has actually improved the enquiry rate. The robo team is far more involved and feels like they are genuinely interested in getting the best results possible. If you already use a bot and pay more than RoboReception, it makes zero sense not to switch. If you don't have one, then you're missing out.

Anon

We have converted all three practices over to RoboReception from a competitor that we were paying three times the amount for. We haven't looked back; leads are great and the integration is top notch!

Anon

We've already had three enquiries in the first day.

Heyford smiles

We are excited to announce we have joined! We're excited to add the amazing feature to our website. Watch this space.

Dinah Nassan

It's an absolutely incredible tool to add to your website. Made by a legend of a dentist for dentists – Grant McAree.

Ahmed Giaziri

Loving RoboReception; it really is as good as Donna and Grant promised. It ain't rocket science. Affordable and value for money.

Anon

ROI is obscene.

How to sort your operations

We are going to create an at-a-glance system for leads. From the advert to the moment the patient arrives, it will track them through their patient journey. This is what it looks like.

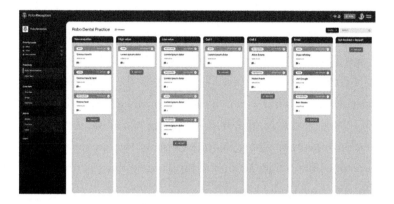

All leads from all sources land in column one. 'All enquiries': Facebook, IG, website, Google ads – all your marketing avenues. They all funnel into column one. At a glance you will be able to see which marketing strategy is working and which one is a failure. It is no longer a feeling but a hard fact!

RoboReception has a really neat little feature – if the lead stays in column one for too long, it turns from green to amber. If it stays there a little longer, guess what happens? You got it! It turns red. So, if all of column one is red, the reception team are not doing their job. If they had contacted the patient, they would have moved the lead to column two! Some dentists like to split the next column into 'low' and 'high' value treatments. The beauty of this operational system is that you can design it how you like, but you are also welcome to copy my template. In fact, we will also help you design it to suit your business.

When the lead finally ends in the clinical column 'First consultation', it is now up to the dentist to show how good they are. They will need to convert that patient to move them to 'Full assessment'. If too many leads build up in the 'First consultation' column, conversion training for the reception team may be required! Now you can see how accountability plays a role in the improvement of your business, and everyone can see the patterns that will emerge.

There's nowhere to hide. They can't say the business doesn't provide leads. They can't say receptionists aren't doing their job. What is this doing? It is providing accountability. It is a demonstration of where there is a hole in the bucket and who is responsible for it. Accountability and analysis is now alive. Oh, welcome to the game!

Examples of the RoboReception LeadTracker in action can be found in the resource page under videos.

Where to start?

The Free Option: Trello

What it is: there is a free version that is fab. It lacks a few clever additions that we made to the RoboReception LeadTracker but it is still very cool. The free version uses Trello (www.trello. com), a personal organiser. This board can be created easily and in any way that suits your patient journey. I introduced

Trello to the dental world as a lead management board in 2015. At my dental practice it took on a life of its own. My staff extended the boards and used it to alert when lab work is in, when ClinChecks had to be done, when consents needed to be signed – a complete memory system. Adding this to my tree, to the Operational branch, felt like a perfect fit. I now use the RoboReception LeadTracker, as it has further trendy little features that I designed to make a dental practice patient journey seamless. For dentists by dentists.

Example of the basic Trello Board template can be found in the *Resource Pack: Task 6*. Download the template and then get building!

The Pro Option: RoboReception LeadTracker

What it is: if you want some special additions – for example, the traffic light system to show how long the lead has been sitting waiting to be contacted, how many leads have dropped in that day and how many leads have been actioned, where the leads have come from, full support and a full design spec – that is what comes with RoboReception. That will be a monthly investment of £99 (plus VAT).

How to get started: visit www.roboreception.co.uk and fill out the contact form. We will design the RoboReception LeadTracker for you. We will upload a free chatbot to your website and train your staff. Full support, no ties. It is seamless. The phrase 'designed by dentists for dentists' sums it up. No more complicated CRM systems that you don't understand. All those figures, columns and added extras that are useless and confusing have been stripped out. *When Donna and I designed the RoboReception LeadTracker we didn't want to lose sight of what dentists needed and would find useful. A design that is over-complicated causes more stress than efficiency. I just want to see where the leads are, when they dropped in (traffic light system) and where the system is working and where it is screwing up. Hence why the RoboReception LeadTracker was created.*

Shall I say again? It is designed by dentists for dentists. Fire a member of staff on Friday and the new team member can be up to speed in ten minutes. And you can see what is going on and where. Full accountability and analysis!

Pro option benefits over the free option:

1. full technical support

2. the integrated RoboReception ChatBot can be uploaded to your website to capture leads and deliver them seamlessly to your RoboReception LeadTracker

3. traffic light system so all team members can be monitored more effectively

4. full design support

5. staff training

6. reports and analysis on request

7. join a growing community sharing ideas

8. 30% discount to all Dental Business and Marketing Courses run by Dr Grant McAree

Summary

And that is it. The one operational arm of the STFD business model: accountability and analysis. When you see where you are broken you will see what to mend. When you see what needs to be fixed, you can fix it. You can then invest in other areas of the business that won't be wasted funds. You won't have a broken chain. They say the chain is as strong as the weakest link. This is the solution.

The next chapters will show how it all ties together. How customers, people and the financial branches of the tree all come together. When you get the hole mended, when you get the bucket in order, let's throw some bloody water in it. Let's fill your boots. I haven't mentioned my strapline much in all the words I have written, although I have been so excited to use it more. It's been like a whisper in my ear and I hope you see it now: all the business stuff, all this business of dentistry, it ain't rocket science!

CHAPTER 7

PEOPLE

My story

I would love to talk about one particular event, one gem that sticks in my memory, but I can't. And why? Because I have so many incidents that I look back on and shudder. Before I adopted my STFD business model, I thought I ruled the world. I thought building a business was about numbers. To me the number of staff I employed was directly related to my success. At meetings I looked at all my staff with pride. Not realising they all thought I was a bit of a bellend. If you look back in life and can't see you were an idiot it is highly likely you are still an idiot. Love that saying! Well, in no uncertain terms – I was an idiot. In no uncertain terms it was down to me, my management, my approach to the staff that caused the issues that I experienced.

I remember having an absolute fear of not being in control. I had to make sure I ruled the roost. On day one, the manager moved the radio from the waiting room to behind reception. I was incensed. I lost sleep that night. One of many nights

If you look back in life
and can't see you were an
idiot it is highly likely you
are still an idiot.

without sleep. If I could look back and know what I know now, know that there would be many sleepless nights over little things like bloody radios, would I still have carried on this journey? Damn right I would. So back to the radio. I see you sitting there thinking why would I get so upset? Such a small thing. But looking back, the radio had nothing to do with what upset me. I was making sure that the manager knew I was the boss. I was the one steering the ship. I reckon I looked like a total pillock, but at the time I was so inexperienced and everything was a series of knee-jerk reactions, and decisions were made from subconscious feelings and thoughts. Similar events happened regularly. Staff would be left confused by my reactions. In a period of six months I lost every member of staff. It was totally 'my bad'. Doh!

It was an eight-surgery powerhouse with 30 members of staff. One of the largest private practices in Devon. I was 29, and I knew bugger all about nurturing a business, let alone sustaining one. When they all left me, one by one, I started to blame everyone else – the affairs that staff were having, the attitude of employees, the lazy culture of the workforce at the time. It was down to me, the way I managed and steered the ship.

One night I was closing up and one of my managers came to me with a bag of cheques. They were found in the toilet. The cash was missing. A staff member had stolen from me. About £400. I was devastated. I felt my world had collapsed. I felt wounded beyond belief because I felt I had provided the ultimate working environment. I never proved who did this, but I know – I definitely know. Karma will get them, but sometimes you just have to move on. However, as I look back, maybe I hadn't provided the environment I thought I had. It is the balance I failed at. The final nail in the coffin was when we went out to dinner – a dental event. The environment I had created was well and truly broken. I had to book two tables so the staff didn't have to associate with each other. There was a clear divide between management and staff, between nurses and reception. The world I had created was a horror show.

The business was everything to me. All my insecurities came flooding back. I seemed to plaster over all my childhood issues by creating this massive business. At the time it gave me confidence. I felt alive. I felt sort of powerful. When it appeared to fall apart, so did I. When something becomes so overwhelmingly crap, depression sets in. You depress all your feelings. You become a bag of nerves.

What kept me going? I was still a millionaire at 29 years old even though the business was falling apart. A bloody miserable one but at least it gave me some confidence that I had achieved something in my life. Just remember that you can run a dental practice and make a lot of money and have no people skills. You can make a load of cash and still have a massive staff turnover. It can happen – it was me! But I was alone in more ways than one.

Through the chain of events, I realised I needed therapy. I couldn't carry on living the life I was living. I wouldn't change anything in my past because of where I am now. However, at that point in time, the people part of my business was a frigging disaster, but it got me to rock bottom. A great place to start swimming back up. I arrived at a dead end. A great place to turn around. If I could say one thing, it would be to get your People branch sorted. For me, it almost got the better of me. However, it turned out to be the main reason for me to develop the Strategy Tree For Dentists! As soon as the People branch of the STFD business model was incorporated into my business, I began to enjoy the job again. The constant struggle to survive subsided. The business of dentistry no longer felt like a chore.

What's this step all about?

If you neglect your working culture, your people will cause you problems. They will rip the soul out of your dreams. In other words, they will be a pain in the arse. If the staff leave or there is bitching, it is incredibly stressful for you as the owner or you as a colleague. The more sensitive you are the more you will pick up on other people's pain and anguish. Team spirit is infectious but so is apathy and bad feeling. Achieve a good working culture and it can improve your business, your life, your well-being. Get it wrong and you may as well pack up and go home.

If you have a situation like I did, with high staff turnover, it's a nightmare. Do you know how much time is spent training a new member of staff? I remember looking back at a new member of staff and thinking it was never an expensive problem to have. However, if you add up all the people hours spent getting the new staff member up to speed, which doesn't even include the advertising costs. Every phone call they take could be lost revenue as they come over unconfident and untrained. When I carry out mystery shops for new clients, I regularly get asked not to do the calls on a particular day as the new girl is on the desk! This is just not good business.

Losing staff and getting a replacement could run into tens of thousands of pounds of lost revenue. And that is just the admin team.

Let us now consider the clinical team. We all know what it is like when we arrive at work and the computer isn't on. The room isn't warm and the lab work isn't out. The notes aren't filled out and the patients aren't called from the waiting room in the way you have become accustomed to. Sorry, in a way you have taken for granted! Suddenly your capacity to earn the targeted daily turnover not only shrinks but it is a nightmare surviving to the end of the day. By home time you are dog tired, irritated and not looking forward to the following day when you know it is going to be just as bad because your golden person is not sitting beside you! Suddenly there is a lot of love for your nurse. You make that promise you are going to be that bit nicer from now on. No matter how much of a crap boss I have been over the years, I have always remembered to say thank you to my team. Lauren Burton, thank you – you are my superstar!

So, in short: what is this all about? Why is it so important to get it right? If you don't get it right, it will cost you not only lost revenue but an incredible amount of stress. Ultimately, your business will either fail or break you. At best you will be building a business that could be so much more. You could be living a far more stress-free life. I lost so much time in my life with not getting this side of the business sorted. If I could go back and talk to myself again it would be to let myself know that this area of business is one of the most important. The most crucial. I don't want to paint a bad picture of dentists. Most businesses are never perfect.

However, if you get it very wrong, you end up paying out in the form of an apology forced on you by a tribunal. I have a friend (not a client) who took a member of staff out to lunch to fire her. A bit like Jerry Maguire. In a crowded restaurant so the team member couldn't make a scene. He proceeded to fire her. She then reported she was pregnant. 'Sorry, I still need you to go.' That one sentence. Seven words. Cost him £12,000 as an apology. That is £1,714 per word! I do want to clarify he didn't lose the tribunal case because she was pregnant. He lost all that dosh because he hadn't followed procedure. He was not aware of the law. The law that rightly protects employees. But point 1 – do not take your staff out to lunch to fire them. Point 2 – re- read point 1, and remember a restaurant is not the place to fire someone just because you think they won't make a scene.

I work for Portman now and I can safely say they are building a great family feel. They are breaking the mould of corporate dentistry. Dentists all think that corporate dentistry is 'the Dark Side' and when I finally sold and started day one as an associate again, I suppose it felt that way. But as I look deeper into how Portman run the show, I found that it made sense. It *is* about the numbers, but I have found an organisation that is *also* about the people. It feels reassuring to be part of that culture. Let me say that again: 'It feels reassuring to be part of that culture.'

I have the ultimate marketing team behind me:

- Derek Uittenbroek – Facebook/IG & Google PPC advertising

- Richard Sproston – SEO & Google My Business

- Donna Hewitt and the RoboReception team.

They do sponsor me, they do pay me, I do use them to get me patients through the door, and I do recommend them; sometimes we dentists do like full disclosure.

I could pick them up and work anywhere after my earn-out with Portman. But I have found myself actually enjoying being part of the family, part of the team.

A happy team is a stable one. A stable team is a happy boss.

Why is it particularly important for dentists wanting to grow?

I think it is crucial that any business nails this branch of the STFD business model. I have developed many businesses. I do feel that dentistry relies heavily on the team more than others. The spotty masturbating YouTube millionaires' only nightmare is if their mum doesn't deliver their tea. For dentistry, all team members play a part, like cogs in a machine. Every cog in the machine has a role to play. If one cog goes, it doesn't work quite so well. It may still function but it just doesn't work so efficiently. The amount of stress caused will be directly proportional to the importance of the cog! So why dentistry?

Dentistry in general

Oh my goodness, what an odd job we have chosen. We work in the smallest part of the body for eight hours at a time. Three inches by three inches. I went on holiday to Cornwall. I met some northern bloke. He had kids in the soft play area next to mine. I asked him what he did for a living. He told me he was an anal specialist. What the hell? I didn't even know one of those specialisms existed. He had this thick Scouse accent. I laughed, as I thought he was joking, so I suppose I discovered we don't work in the smallest part of the body but certainly one of them. This lends itself to quite an intense and stressful environment. You could do without worrying about unhappy staff members and training new members of the team.

We also have an intense requirement for total concentration in that small area. We work next to nerves and blood vessels. One slip and you are deep in the mire – not literally like the anal specialist. With our heads down and the level of concentration required, we rarely look up. It is this lack of looking up that means that we can miss so many problems that are percolating: a member of staff being bullied, a team member causing trouble, a receptionist being rude on the phone or a receptionist who has recently got a tattoo on their forehead. If you already have a poor working culture, the dental business is almost a breeding ground for assholes. They can run riot and rip the very heart out of any thriving business.

The dentist and nurse relationship

What an odd relationship this is. What other business do you know where two members of the team work so closely together for so long? You, the nurse and the patient, all of you intruding on each other's personal space. It's an invasion of personal boundaries, and with this invasion comes trust. If there is no trust then this relationship breaks down so quickly. Even down to where to put your legs!

I remember back in the day (I feel old when I say that) that dental nurses all had to wear dresses. I received a complaint from a dental nurse. The dentist insisted on putting his left knee in between the legs of the dental nurse whilst they worked on a patient. Shock horror, I hear you say, but it makes sense. The dental nurse can then move in closer to aspirate. Personally, I think this is a shocking invasion of the nurse's personal boundaries and I don't care how big your balls are, close your legs and allow your nurse to sit alongside you. Again, this personal invasion of boundaries is about trust. If that trust is gone then the dentist will lose a nurse quicker than they can say sorry.

When your nurse has gone, do you know how much revenue could be lost? Oh my, I have seen it. The average dentist will lose £10k a month gross whilst training up a newbie. Having the right instruments ready and having that lab work on the side when you need it are things we all take for granted, but when it's gone you suddenly miss that assistant who could almost read your mind. I won't even mention the stress it takes to train and nurture a new dental nurse.

Dentists and partnerships

I have never taken on a dental business partner. Never have, never will. I see them failing everywhere. They are good friends as they start out, full of enthusiasm, full of hope. The friendship rarely survives a dental partnership. It nearly broke my father and I've seen the same pattern in so many practices. Why do dental partnerships fail? In my opinion, it is about staff culture and money.

There is inevitable jealousy if one of the partners earns more money or is more likable. They don't get to spend time with each other to sustain a friendship or healthy partnership as they are both busy treating patients. The biggest issue is they weren't taught business at university. They are thrust into that business world with no clue how to run it. They create a poor working culture that breeds gossiping resulting in a rapid decline in team spirit. When that is coupled with the fact that dentists are down in the mouth eight hours a day, I personally think partnerships are doomed to fail. Not all, though! I think the ones that survive – for example, the Smile Clinic Group, those talented well-driven fellas – know how to motivate their team, and what a first-class working culture they have created. Hats off to Jin Vaghela and Kish Patel. I look at them and a George Burns song comes to mind – 'Oh I wish I was 18 again'.

Your stress

I am sure we all know what it means for the day-to-day running of the practice when one person shouts, 'One person down.' The first thoughts I always had were, 'Skiving so and so. Why are they ill again? Can't they just have a work ethic like me? They are so bloody lazy. Can't they just come and sit at reception? Can they sit in the back room and answer the phone? I am certainly not paying them, get another member of staff in off their holiday.'

Then you're struck by the realisation of how awful the day is without a full team. There is the real cost to the business when the team does not function at 100%. We all run around like idiots trying to fill in. Phones don't get answered, more lost revenue. No wonder we hate people going off sick. Stress and loss of income. A poor work culture means sickness rates will go up. That is a well-known fact. A positive working culture, where people enjoy their jobs, will mean that they will do everything they possibly can to get into work and not create a stress for the team.

Patients

Equally important are the patients. They don't want to visit a practice where there are miserable faces and bitching. A bad atmosphere will be felt by your customers. They are nervous enough without having to experience a bad atmosphere. I have dealt with many complaints in my time. A common one that kept cropping up was from patients saying the nurse had been treated badly by a moody dentist dishing out their stress!

Over the years, on many occasions, patients have complained that the nurse was crying due to a dentist being short and giving their chairside assistant the blame for treatment that had not gone to plan. If you are one of those dentists, shame on you. I need to clarify this point, though – if you have had a bit of an argument, and one of you ends up in tears and an apology follows, that is all part of the human experience. However, there is no place for bullying under my roof. Never has been, never will be. I have also lost patients because of these interactions between the dentist and the nurse. The atmosphere became so awkward that the patient refused to return. A patient lost is a lifetime of revenue down the toilet. Create a positive workforce and these issues are simply not tolerated from the outset.

In short...

A positive work culture and a good atmosphere within your dental practice will mean everyone benefits. The patients, your staff and, above all, your bank balance! It is no secret that the dental profession is changing rapidly. The strain on the NHS and the effects of the Covid crisis are clear – the entire dental industry is under strain. Nurses have left the profession. Hundreds of dental nurses refused to return after Covid (in July 2021, the GDC's figures show that 3,826 dental nurses didn't renew their registrations at the end of that month). The job just became too damn hard. A shortage of nurses means an increase in demand on wages for the ones that are left behind. So, for goodness' sake, look after the ones who are still standing by your side. They are gold dust and should be treated as such because when they are gone, they are gone.

Client Story: The Power of D.E.S.C

I feel very privileged to be in this position, writing a book. I am filled with fear about the thought of releasing it! In truth, it is almost like therapy. It makes me realise I am not the only dentist who struggled and suffered with staff, making the same mistakes as I did. The stress caused by staff in my career has almost finished me off at different times along the way. I would say that they are the number one cause of broken businesses. As you read through this book you will see I have made many mistakes, but sometimes we just find ourselves up against it, employing members of the team who turn out to be untrainable – or maybe they were just hell bent on being assholes from the get-go.

What was happening? What was going wrong?

One client particularly resonated with me. A manager. We shall call him Clive. He contacted me out of sheer desperation. In truth, he was almost broken. The staff didn't listen to him, the principal went about his merry way and dropped in now and again to bark a few orders, undermining Clive's attempts at managing and making decisions. The famous Chinese proverb 'the fish rots from the head' was so true in Clive's case. Money was being thrown at the manager to go on more courses, but the staff were out of control. One of the nurses had started an OnlyFans. Receptionists had very little guidance on uniform so would turn up scruffy. Any decisions to discipline staff were based on knee-jerk reactions without any support from the top. There was a managers' meeting but it was infrequent and rarely effective in dealing with all the issues. In fact, the meetings were a total waste of time. Promises were made by management, but nothing was followed up. So, in short, it was just a get-together that was considered a total waste of time. Was the principal there? No, they were out playing golf and driving fast cars.

One meeting brought it all to a head. The manager had arranged the seats so all the staff could be positioned in a circle. The seat number was incorrectly accounted for. One short. As the manager got up to make a coffee one of the nurses jumped in his seat and refused to move. Shouted out it was probably a good idea for the manager to stand. How totally disrespectful. It was nearly the end for Clive, and I tell you this: what is more devastating is the business had massive potential. It had patients falling over themselves to visit the surgery. This wasn't the post-Covid rush – this was the norm. The location of the surgery and the skills of the dentists kept the patients coming through the door despite high staff turnover, and despite threats being made to Clive by certain members of staff.

One dentist said that they would leave if their nurse didn't get a pay rise. I would love to have got my gloves on and walked into that clinic to ask them what on earth it had to do with them. But I couldn't. It wouldn't have made any difference. It would have just caused grief. Maybe my staff thought I was a bit of a dick, but they would never cross me or be disrespectful to my face. My power to defend was as sharp as a knife. You mess with me and watch out, I will be there ready to take on anyone, but Clive was too timid. I do think there needs to be a balance between Clive and me, a happy middle ground where respect is the driver, not fear, but it doesn't matter how balanced you are as a manager, you do need the support of your line manager or, in Clive's case, the owner.

When I first spoke to Clive, he was ready to jump ship. We had a conversation about him starting his own dental business around the corner from the practice. I hope this hits home, readers. This manager had a fire in their belly. They had been in the business for so long they knew it inside-out. They wanted to take the legs out from the principal who was lazy, unsupportive and absent. That owner would have been left scratching their heads wondering how it all went so very wrong. Their cars sold, their golf trips cut short. That business was ready to implode.

Where did we start?

I got a pencil and pen out and listened. We have two ears and one mouth for a reason. Shut up and listen. You will never learn anything by speaking, only by listening. We listed all the issues, and there were many. It all came out. How alone Clive was, how literally powerless he felt when dealing with problems. The lack of support resulted in knee-jerk reactions that never resulted in an action being taken. There was zero support from the top.

What did I do/advise?

Firstly, we needed to buy Clive some time to breathe and to make sure that there was support. That was halfway to sorting this mess out. My advice to anyone who finds themselves in a similar position to Clive is to make sure you have a quiet moment to reflect on any decision or confrontation. From that point on, Clive had a saying, 'Let me just put that on the boil, let it simmer, I will get back to you.' Clive didn't have to say it out loud but it bought him that extra bit of time needed to think about an answer when confronted by a staff member who had questions that could not be answered at that very moment. Anxiety and stress make you try to resolve problems the moment they surface, but this is not the ideal way to tackle business problems, especially in the dental world! Before long, Clive managed to get staff to email him any issues so he had time to reflect and work out a solution.

The second issue was the problem with the principal. This was slightly more of an issue. It wasn't so much the absence that was the problem, it was the total lack of support; a lot of Clive's decisions were being overruled, which was undermining Clive and leading to the staff disrespecting him too. The prospect of Clive approaching the owner literally terrified him, so I taught Clive the D.E.S.C tactic. It is not only powerful but it is an approach that cannot be argued with. It cannot be challenged, as it is real. It is based on fact. It is based on feeling. This is how it goes.

D

This is for describing. This is a fact. Let's call the owner Derek. Clive was to describe to Derek the events that existed. The true facts. Not flowering it up. 'Derek, you are not here in the business to support me regularly, and you overrule my decisions.' Derek cannot argue with this. He isn't in the business, so there is no possible pushback against that comment.

E

This is for effect. The effect this is having on Clive. 'When you are not here and supporting me, it makes me feel alone. I feel staff do not respect my decisions. I feel that I am in the middle with no one to turn to.' Again, this is a comment that Derek cannot argue with. It is a feeling Clive is experiencing and only a narcissist could try to refute this approach.

S

This is for specific. Be specific. This is when you are defining your needs. What you want. The changes you want to make and the changes you want to see in the other person. 'I want you to support me more. I want you to support the decisions I make. I am happy to run them all by you if you give me time, but whether you are in the business in person or not, you need to be standing by my side.' Again, this is clear and assertive.

C

This is for consequence. This part of the resolution process takes confidence. You also have to see it as a promise to yourself. If you say it, you mean it. 'If you do not support me, I am going to rip this business apart and set up down the road, and I will be driving your frigging sports car, you utter lazy shite.' Or you remain calm! 'If you do not support me, I will have to leave the business, as I am tired and I have simply had enough.'

Clive's result

This phone call took only two hours but resulted in so much change. I followed up a month later. I couldn't believe the difference. Two small elements of the business that needed to be changed. They didn't need to spend thousands of pounds a month on support. Like a toothache – they needed an assessment, diagnosis and a plan! A plan that was carried out with marine accuracy. Don't get me wrong, this was one story in hundreds I could talk about, but it's one that sticks in my mind. A simple adjustment can make a business thrive – ignoring Clive's requests could have broken the business in two. Don't get me wrong – Derek is still golfing and driving stupidly expensive cars, but when he is present, he is present, supporting and guiding Clive. Look at the power of the People branch of the STFD.

How to start sorting your people out

When someone calls me, it is usually out of desperation, as they are at the point of breaking. They are almost looking over the cliff edge. They have had enough and are ready to jump ship. I think it is down to one thing: the lack of power. Now, I am not talking about being a control freak. I am talking about a total lack of power over your team. The lack of ability to guide the ship. A poor working culture has led to poor decisions and a lack of direction by everybody. The hardest thing in life is change. Change scares not only the person driving those changes but the staff on the receiving end. Staff will push back, they will feel vulnerable, if only for a short while. Support and reassurance will be required. You will need to be the iron fist in the velvet glove. You will need to be strong yet caring, you will need to reach out without being a rescuer. You will need to be assertive without being the villain. You will need to ask for support without being a victim.

Step 1: Get lawyered up

I don't mean start sending letters out and being threatening. I mean make sure you are on the right side of the law! Get help, get the correct advice. HR is an enormous minefield. A self-employed associate has very different rights to the employed receptionist. If you treat a dentist with a self-employed contract in the same way as your employed admin team – for example, you begin disciplinary procedures if you catch them snogging the hygienist – they can make a claim you are employing them and then you may end up owing all their back taxes! Get a good company who can advise you if and when issues arise.

Step 2: Interview well

The interview is the first hello. I remember my staff banned me from interviews when I started out. I didn't realise there was a process. Legal steps you have to take and timings with regard to providing the contract is crucial. I once sat in a room interviewing for a nurse position. I asked the interviewee the reasons for leaving their last position. They said it was because they had been caught shagging with the boss. I was 29 years old! How was I supposed to deal with that response? I dealt with it very badly. I think a drop of snot came out my nose at one point, and I nearly passed out trying to hold in my laugh. That moment was a defining moment for me – I never sat in on an interview again.

Step 3: Provide the right information to everybody

You can employ an HR company, as they are not very expensive. They will also support you in any legal argument as long as you follow their advice.

If you choose to go it alone and employ staff without any advice or guidance, make sure you provide every member of staff with the following documents.

1. Statement of main terms and conditions. Most dentists only provide this. It is not sufficient. Many of us call this 'the contract'. Please remember the word 'contract' is not a collective noun for the handbook and job description. A contract is a legally binding document. We also advise clients not to have handbooks and job descriptions in the contract because of this fact.

2. The job description. This explains what they have to do and how. This can be changed. How they answer the

phone, what you expect from them in their role. This can be a development in process.

3. The handbook. This covers other stuff! It covers hygiene, dress code and many other areas of dentistry an owner wants to keep a tight control over.

All these documents are provided separately. They give a clear indication of where the ship is going, how you want it steered, who is steering it and how fast. It gives you the ultimate control over your business. Without it you are sailing in a storm, in the dark with no sails or crew. I have seen a multi-million-pound dental practice cave in overnight because of one bad apple (that member of staff who is hell bent on being an asshole – we have all had one or two of those over the years). They can tear the place inside out by making an accusation. It finished a dentist I know. All they had worked for. The accusation turned out to be false but the damage was done. Get the start right and the rest falls into place. The three documents show you mean business and what is expected in no uncertain terms.

Step 4: Monitor staff development

When the staff member starts, they will be in their honeymoon period. They are as sweet as an angel. So, many times over my career, I have sat back proud of myself for picking such a diamond. No one has discovered this little gem sitting at the reception desk. They can sell, answer the phone, they just do their thing. Staff like them and they are helpful, then their feet get under the table and they settle in. They become a nightmare overnight. Argumentative and abrupt. You suddenly realise why they were unemployed when they walked through your door. They then become a nightmare to get rid of, so make sure you have regular six-monthly reviews. Monitor and watch them like a hawk!

Step 5: Keep in touch

Morning huddles, practice meetings and of course nights out. I used to take my team to a local nightclub. I paid for the entire evening. I managed to get so much information about the business. It gelled the team. One business took his staff to Spain once a year. How cool is that!

I do want to mention this morning huddle. Some call it a morning hug. Don't make it a coffee morning chit-chat about bugger all. I have seen the most badly run practices claiming they had these morning hugs! Total waste of everyone's time. May as well be in clinic. Have a structure to the chats, even if it is in your head! It shouldn't be about the weekend drunken stories. Business is business. In my day, it was about gaps in the diaries, problems on reception. Yes, have a hug – but make it count!

Step 6: Keep staff motivated

We do talk a lot about bonuses and how to keep the team motivated. They are a bloody disaster half the time and rarely work. Why? In my opinion, they are poorly thought-out. Yes, money is a good motivator but not the only driving force.

We have discussed the five passions, and it is the same for staff members. If you throw money at a staff member who has a passion to bond and feel, they will get bored with you throwing money at them as a motivator. They may want time off with their family and loved ones as a gift for their hard work. They will sit back and let others work for the extra pennies, but they will then get criticised for doing nothing.

A poorly thought-out bonus scheme can break the team rather than build a positive work culture. Other members of staff may have a passion to learn. They may want to have a course paid for or tuition fees covered. My point is that money is not everyone's goal! (I never understood that, but it is unfortunately true!) A good bonus scheme will consider everyone's passions.

Step 7: Be appreciative (don't take staff for granted)

Like I said, always thank your nurse and reception team every day! Maybe a gift, the occasional envelope with some money in it. Even the ones who don't have a passion to acquire will appreciate the thought! They take home the same stresses as you. Appreciate your nurses – if you are one of those bullies who blames the nurse when you have screwed up – well, that makes you a special kind of plonker. If you don't want to stick your hand in your pocket (that includes associates), buy the team a bloody cake. I don't understand it when I see associates so bloody stingy. You earn £100K a year! Share a bit of love around. It isn't only the principal that should be doing this.

Exercise

We all love those six-monthly reviews! Why don't you take it one step further? Takes a lot of courage, though! The 360-degree feedback exercise. Basically, the recipient (the principal) gets feedback from all directions! Bloody nightmare. Back in the day I was found to be unapproachable and defensive. It hurt like nobody's business. I felt the staff were so bloody ungrateful. In truth, it did reshape the way I managed staff and it turned my business around. I look back and realise I was very much how I was assessed. I am grateful to this day that I carried out this very uncomfortable exercise.

I have provided a 360-degree feedback form in the *Resource Pack: Task 7*.

Summary

I do think that the staff are the life of the business. One bad apple can cripple you. One good apple can pull the team along. The fish does rot from the head down. If the lead clinician has their head down and fails to spot problems or chooses to ignore the difficult members of staff then it can be catastrophic. The hardest challenge when developing a business is to manage a prickly over-sensitive member of staff. It can be terrifying. I used to walk into reception and creep back out, as I couldn't bear the way the receptionist was talking on the telephone. That was before I decided to have a better life and before I wanted to improve the way I conducted myself. In fact, it was before I invented the STFD business model. If you develop a structure and a process and give clear direction (and of course have the law on your side) anything is possible. You will have what everyone wants – you will have what we all dream about on a Monday morning: you will have 'the Dream Team'.

CHAPTER 8

CUSTOMER

My story

Have I always had the perfect patient journey? The perfect customer care? Have I hell. I have dropped the baton, had a broken chain, holes in the bucket, I have bled patients from not creating the environment I now know I am capable of building today. It makes me shudder to think just how crap my customer care was at times. I was oversensitive and punchy. I failed regularly to appreciate the fear patients felt when they visited the dentist.

Today, if one of my associates or one of my staff demonstrates poor customer care, it is my problem, my issue and ultimately my responsibility. So, when did I know I had to make a change? When did the penny drop? It was a few months into running my own business. I got a complaint letter about my treatment. The first cut is the deepest, a bit like the first scratch you make on that new car. The first one always hurts and wounds more deeply.

I hadn't explained the issues with the treatment or the possible side effects that could happen. The receptionist asked for money upfront and was not polite. The toilet had crap stains on the bowl after another patient had used it. Yes, you read that correctly. A complaint about a sly turd that hadn't been cleaned off the toilet. Maybe a little over the top, but when I really dug deep and looked at the processes in place, that patient had a right to be unhappy. The complaint letter had not been answered in a timely manner. There was no understanding of the patient's issues. Patients have a right to voice their concerns, but if the top person (me) is defensive and insensitive to the patient's fears and concerns, a lack of empathy will drift through the practice.

I then started analysing the language we used on reception. The following is a list of many sayings I heard on my watch, in my business, on a daily basis.

- *You need to* book an appointment.
- *You have to* pay a deposit.
- *You have to* come back next week.
- *We don't treat* the NHS.
- *Can I have* your name?
- *Fill out* your details.
- *You must* book in for a consultation first.
- *I need* your details.

The above sayings are very common in the dental industry. When I started to develop a more positive customer care strategy, I began to think they were aggressive and verging on rude – at best, abrupt! I recall on many occasions I would walk into the reception area and the admin team would be on the phone. I would be horrified by the way the patients were being talked to. I would walk back out too scared to approach the staff member as they frightened the crap out of me, too! Was I frightened? Bloody right I was. I lived in fear of a moody sulk for three days or that a confrontation would get ugly resulting in the staff member handing in their notice. In truth, it was my weakness and inability to resolve issues. A lack of confidence.

When I started dentistry, it wasn't the same sue culture. I remember being threatened with court action one day in the clinic, to which I replied, 'I would welcome the challenge.' I realise now how dentistry has changed. How it has become far more patient focused. In short, we are so vulnerable and have to accept so much abuse from patients as we are so highly regulated and the fear of losing our jobs weighs us down on a daily basis. So, I suppose customer care had to improve. But, to be fair, I never had the time! I was working on mouths, so how did I have the time to check on reception? Yes, I carried out a mystery shop once to check out the responses from an enquiry. It turned out to be a total disaster. It was recorded. I actually ended up ignoring the result and it was literally a train wreck. The receptionist failed at everything. They didn't ask the patient's name, where they heard of the business, they didn't build rapport or even know the prices. They directed the poor patient to the website. I was devastated. The realisation struck that I had built a powerhouse, but one with terrible customer care. It could have been so much better, so much bigger and with greater profits and a happier and more well-trained team. It was down to me, my responsibility, and I totally accept it was my failure.

This branch of the STFD business model is about customer care. Ensuring your paying customer is treated so well that they want to return again and again. *It can take months to find a customer but seconds to lose one* (Vince Lombardi). Get those seconds right! Make sure the body language and verbal interactions are warm and inviting and not crude and demanding.

I saw a question on my Facebook page, The Dental Business and Marketing Group. A dentist liked to stir things up by asking questions that started a debate. He asked: 'Is the gift of the gab more important than excellent technical skills?' Of course, the gift of the gab is the most important; patients don't have a clue what a good dentist is. Like I said, a good dentist to the majority of the public is upper canine to canine – make sure that looks good and, whilst you do the dental treatment, make it as painless as possible. So, make sure that, if you want a business to survive, you have the gift of the gab! In other words, make sure your customer care is second to none. If you are stressed out with dentistry, there is nothing worse than unhappy staff, but when you have unhappy patients as well it just adds to the stress. Moaning patients lay heavy on the soul. Dealing with complaints is a nightmare!

Think about it... 50 years ago there was the NHS. Free treatment. Dentists did not advertise so the dental receptionist could be as miserable as the GP receptionist. There was no pressure, no urgency for change and development. There was no demand to be better than the dentist down the road. As the private dental industry started to boom, then patients were presented with more choice. It was with this choice that dentists had the option to either improve or stay within the safe umbrella of the NHS. I am not saying all NHS practices have poor customer care, far from it. Bridget and Malcolm

Prideaux from Plymouth provided a tip-top customer care regardless of whether private or NHS, as did my mother and father. However, as a general rule of thumb, private treatment meant the patient expected more and the dentist was required to fulfil those expectations or lose their patients and see a reduction in their goodwill value.

Why is it important for dentists wanting to grow?

Here is my list of reasons why your customer care has to be spot on when considering opening a dental business.

It will keep your business going in quiet or difficult times. If you want to keep your businesses afloat, I don't mean the post-Covid rush, or when the NHS collapse underpins a crappy private service, I mean in difficult times when everyone is fighting for business, then you must get that customer care spot on! This is when the practices with the top-notch customer care will survive and thrive. They will sweep up all those patients. In hard times patients become choosier, and they become more demanding. They have a choice. That choice has consequences. The consequences being that the businesses providing poor customer care will miss out.

Forget the difficult times – if you don't look after your customers, don't expect them to stick around, even when there is an abundance of patients and a shortage of dentists. If you fall behind in the customer care department, you will end up wondering how those appointment books that were rammed full have suddenly developed cracks and spaces. From eight weeks fully booked, it can quickly diminish to booking up a few days in advance. I see it with my competitors today. Patients come to see me now from all over the South West. I hear stories about how my competitors deal with new patients. They forget to give them plans, follow up phone calls, they are rude and uncaring, shocking bedside manners. The one result is always the same – universal – the patient will always seek out someone else to provide a better service.

Regulars are truly valuable. Have you considered how much someone will spend in a basic run-of-the-mill dental practice? I am talking about a business that provides general dentistry. Now calculate the average yearly spend and then multiply that by 30. They could be with you for 30 years. Then their parents, their children. You make a comfortable visit for the nervous patient and you will have them for life. That is more profitable than a dental implant or an Invisalign brace provided for a transient type of patient.

People are frightened to visit the dentist. Dentistry is rated in the top seven most extreme of phobias. Patients need to feel comfortable and relaxed, not only to spend money but to remain a loyal patient.

If the customer care is spot on it is infectious. It will rebound off patients and staff. It will create a working environment where there is less sickness, more happy faces and greater profit. It is the missing link in the chain. It can transform a basic practice into a supercharged business worth millions!

It makes life easier. I always found sales easier if the customer care was spot on. Dentists found selling easier and reception found asking for money more comfortable. It becomes a well-oiled machine. There is also an improvement in efficiency, as there is less time wasted trying to fix the problems that happen when a patient is treated badly.

Good customer care represents trust. Trust is so desperately needed for the patient and dentist relationship to work effectively (my son, Josh, told me that, and he is only 16 years old!). Customers should think that we genuinely care about their well-being.

It helps you make better marketing decisions. You can then establish where to put future budgets, where you can concentrate on better and more effective advertising strategies. The holes in the buckets are getting fixed! If you get 100 patients through the door and you then lose them all due to poor customer care then you will never know if it is due to the staff turning the patients away or your advert targeting! Knee-jerk marketing investments are killers to the profit!

May I say one final point! Manners cost nothing. Make sure your staff have good manners! It is the first step. The customer care branch of the STFD business model – the one powerful bucket plugger, chain fixer – it doesn't cost a penny. And we dentists do love a freebie.

Client Story: The Impact of Mystery Shoppers

What was happening and what was going wrong?

When I think back to how I have helped many clients, the one area that always needs improvement across the board is customer care. As stated, 99% of our mystery shops were shockingly bad last year! Staggering, really. So, when James called me and said his business was failing, we started there!

James phoned me out of desperation. He had a seven-surgery practice in South East UK. With seven clinical rooms, it took a fair bit of cash on a monthly basis. They had a mixed list – NHS and private. In my opinion, it is hard to run a mixed practice. Splitting NHS and private waiting rooms, treatment times and types of service are recipes for disaster. Either treat them all the same (providing an amazing NHS service equal to private) or don't run a mixed practice. It may be possible to make those paying private patients feel special, but those NHS patients are equally as loud, equally, if not more, demanding, and equally capable of writing a crappy Google review.

James still insisted on the NHS private mix and wanted to provide a cracking service for his fee-paying private patients. He wanted tea and coffee in a relaxed lounge with nice smelling air filters and magazines. James had a goal, a vision. His present system was failing terribly. It created resentment amongst staff and patients. The private nurses and reception team seemed to distance themselves from their NHS colleagues in the practice. The dentists were all moaning that they didn't earn enough or that new patients were not shared out equally. Nurses were getting complaints. Patients were leaving. It was by no means anyone's fault. The customer care was poor but that was the result of a split and divide within the business, which was devastating to see and equally devastating to the business and James's finances.

What did I do/advise?

Please remember it is rarely a one-fix job-done. I supported the business for six months with mystery shops, analysis of the finances and patient conversion rates. The list was endless but crucial towards making an assessment, a diagnosis and a plan to fix the broken links.

The first stop was the mystery shop. I phoned up and asked the receptionist the cost of their implants. First question. There was no rapport built, no questions, not even a request for my name. The cost was blurted out, approximately £3,000, and I was told that 'you have to book an appointment.' I had to book an appointment! No s***, Sherlock – I thought I would be able to do the treatment remotely! I am only teasing here, but they did say that and that was what was ingrained in them to say. Telling someone that they have to book an appointment is forceful and without feeling and understanding, especially without getting to know the patient on the other side of the phone and without building rapport. The next stage meant I had a look under the bonnet.

Secondly, we put in a CRM system (RoboReception LeadTracker) and discovered the conversion rates for reception were poor and one of the associates (the most difficult and demanding of the team) was even worse. So, out of 100 enquiries 12 went forward with treatment. When I revealed my findings, James went apeshit. I actually thought he was going to break the place up. When he calmed down and made a plan, the positivity shone through.

To begin with, the receptionist was instructed **not** to readily talk about money. They were encouraged to discuss options and provide information, taught to ask questions and nurture the potential enquiry. This is the essence of rapport building. Most patients are not money driven. However, most patients begin with a price question. How much is an implant, how much is Invisalign? I do not advise holding back, or hiding the price. We must be open and transparent. Our prices must be displayed on the website and in the waiting room, clear and certainly not misleading. But consider this – consider the Purchasing Ladder of Awareness:

The Ladder

1. I don't have a problem
2. I have a problem
3. I see you treat this
4. I see you have a solution
5. I see the benefits
6. I am ready to buy

When patients ring the surgery, it may be that they just want a check-up, so they are only at level 1. Do you think they are wanting the £3k price thrown at them at that point? Those incredibly annoying phone recordings whilst you wait, telling patients about discounts, are a bad idea for that very reason! The next patient has broken a tooth, so the patient now has a problem. They may think the implant is an option so they ring up and they are at level 2. The level 2 patients are still not ready for a massive price quote for treatment, even though they think they know what they need! They may need a bridge or a crown! It isn't for the reception team to establish a plan and attach a price accordingly!

In truth, a £3k treatment plan should be advised when the patient is at level 5 or 6! When they can see the benefit of your plan and are ready to buy. And where will the patient be when that happens? You got it! They are in the dental chair! So, James discussed ways the reception could build rapport without advising the price at hello. Suddenly, the new enquiries turned into patients.

Thirdly, we turned our attention to the dentists. Yes, they pushed back but, with the help of the HR company, they had no choice. (I won't go into the self-employed/employed argument – associates are all employed, we all know that!) We designed the surgery layout and we went through ways to convert patients using customer care tips and tricks. And guess what? Revenue went up, associates were happy, patients flooded in and enquiries went up due to word of mouth. I occasionally phone up and ask the price of an implant. The techniques I taught them are still in place. They use other little tips they have found useful, too. The tips and tricks that are the most effective are the ones that make the caller have a more positive experience. That is usually based around getting the caller to chat about themselves.

I don't use reception scripts. I hate bloody scripts. Scripts crush the personality, they prevent the soul from shining through. You want natural, kind, caring staff on the end of a phone not a bloody robot. Give a member of staff a script and they will behave in exactly the way you have instructed them to – cardboard, dull and lifeless.

I finally persuaded James to consider the two-tier system – NHS/Private. Either lift the NHS customer care so they shout at the rooftops about you or convert everyone to private. I remember I transferred 16,000 patients out of the NHS contract to private! That was an entertaining week, but since I have been there and done it I know the pitfalls!

I think the take-home message is: if your staff and patients are happy, the customer care seems to go hand in hand. Create a healthy environment for your staff (including your self-employed dental associates) then the rest seems to follow!

As soon as the customer care improved, so did James's confidence. At that point he decided to drop the NHS contract. This takes massive amounts of courage as it is like severing a lifeline. A nice monthly fee gone in a blink of an eye. But James and I knew he could do it. The extra time could be spent seeing private patients. Nurturing patients up the purchasing ladder of awareness.

We went through different options for patients to purchase dental treatment. Remember, if you are planning to go private, provide choice. Choice is what drives patients to your door. Offer one payment option only and it is like slamming the door shut with them on the outside. Give a choice of a plan, an affordable check-up, pay as you go, patient finance. It will demonstrate you are wanting to make it as easy as possible for them to pay in their own way, their preferred route! This is a positive customer care culture. Welcome to the game! James went private and guess what? He never looked back.

As soon as James went private, more associates applied for the jobs he advertised. Nurses appreciated the slower pace with the customer care they longed to provide but didn't have

If your staff and patients
are happy, the customer
care seems to go hand
in hand.

the time in their previous fast-paced practices. I have heard that some dentists still treat 50 patients a day! How can you hold a hand, ask how the patient is and what their lives are like outside the dental chair? This is how trust is built and rapport is developed. If you have a five-minute check-up, the possibilities to bond with your patient disappear. That is one of the tragedies of NHS dentistry. Time is something that the NHS dentists simply don't have.

When the UDA system came in, I transferred my patients overnight. It was scary, but if you have the customer care, patients will believe in you! So, I appreciated James's fear. But he did it and for that I respected him enormously. And he now enjoys his job again! Let me say that again: James now enjoys his job again. I have spoken to many dentists who are burnt out, bored, stressed, just had enough of drilling holes. Get back to doing the job you like in the way you like doing it! Get that customer care spot on and you can steer your ship straight into the wind and your patients will be loyal! Get it wrong and they will jump ship quicker than the time it took to adjust the sails.

How to improve your customer care

I developed the STFD business model because it was a neat, tidy package. Almost a box diagram. This is how I approached the customer care in my business. This is how I coach dentists who want to improve their businesses – in neat, tidy boxes. The boxes represent different stages along the patient journey, and each box can be independently reviewed and analysed.

The patient journey is influenced by your customer care. If the customer care breaks down along that journey or the baton is dropped then the patient is lost forever. What goes with them is a lifetime of lost revenue. Remember, you please one patient they will tell three others, you annoy them and they will tell ten. That was an old saying when I first started out in dentistry. Today they can tell millions of people how utterly shite you are in one post. It is the harsh reality of modern-day dentistry and the influence of social media. Facebook, Instagram and Google are certainly double-edged swords when it comes to business development!

The Customer Care Patient Journey (my take) is everything after the advert has managed to hook an enquiry.

Step 1: Improve how you respond to online enquiries

Did you know that if you respond to a potential client within two hours apparently you have 50% more chance of them booking in? Oh, shut up. Who on earth has the time to respond at 2am to some drunk fella asking you how much whitening is and does it hurt? My advice – just make sure you respond and don't leave them hanging for days. I do all my own responses and I have template responses for everything! Just remember, make them think you have written the response out just for them! Take a bit of time to respond. No one can write a ten-page response in five minutes. In all my template responses I include everything. So, if someone asks for the price of whitening, I give them everything on whitening: costs, results, whether it hurts, the fact they can pay monthly. The trick is, though, in the template leave a space for their name at the top and a few places within the body of the template. That way they think it has been created just for them! There are neat little tricks for adding these templates into Instagram. I will provide my templates in the *Resource Pack: Task 8*.

I have also provided my template email replies to patients that can be customised. You can find them in the *Resource Pack: Task 9*.

The aim is to get the patient's telephone number so you can contact them and do your thing! I also use an online booking system, particularly if my adverts produce overwhelming responses and requests for bookings. I run an open day deal constantly. It ticks many of my colleagues off. Ask me another question: do I care? Of course not. If you are not upsetting someone you are doing it all wrong. The patient then books online and is asked for a £10 fully refundable deposit. This ensures the patients who book in turn up and are a little higher on the purchasing ladder. Note: I didn't say the lead was bad or poor. I will save that terminology for bellends.

Step 2: Perfect your response to a telephone enquiry

This is where 99% of dental practices fail. I would say it is slightly higher for GP practices. They are rubbish 100% of the time. So here is my secret. Just ask five questions. I don't care what those five questions are, I just want five.

Go to the *Resource Pack: Task 10* to discover some questions that can be asked, but please do not use them like a script. They are just ideas. Encourage staff to think up their own questions! Empower them!

It diverts the patient away from all the cost questions and helps build rapport. Why? Because everyone likes to talk about themselves. We all do! We learn all sorts about our patients as they become relaxed and more likely to book. They believe we are listeners and we think before we jump to a diagnosis. It creates trust.

The questions can be anything. Where they like to go on holiday, what type of dogs they have, do they hate the dentist? There are so many possibilities and options to build trust and to show you are the number one customer care practice in the area. The five questions must not include: where they heard of the practice, name, age, address etc as these are necessary to register the patient. I want five extra! And the icing on the cake: write it as a pop up for the clinical staff to consider.

There are other little points I include when I train reception. Stop using: you must, you have to, I need to take your name. Consider how we talk to customers and remember choice. If you are asking for a deposit, don't say, 'You need to pay for half of your treatment up front', alternatively, 'Would you like to pay for half or all of your next appointment?' Don't say, 'We need to take a deposit before we book an appointment', instead try, 'A deposit is required for you to book an appointment. How would you like to pay for this?' So, in short, provide the patient with a choice; as long as both choices suit you as the owner, who cares? I used to type these responses up and place them as a reminder behind reception, but the amazing customer care providers (the reception team) catch on pretty quickly. The choice approach is huge! The 'choice approach' I am particularly proud of developing. This USP – my USP – shines through in all the businesses I have developed.

Step 3: Perfect your consultation

I only do a three day week. When asked how I manage to convert my patients I always put it down to the fact that I can see through the patient's eyes, see what they see, feel what they are feeling. How do I do that? I just shut up and listen.

Being a dentist, I know what it is like on Friday when we are tired and want to get off home. Consultations become less enthusiastic. The conversion rates are always far lower at the end of the day or even more dire at the end of the week! So, I have a mnemonic for those times, a sort of prop in my head to help me when I am not feeling so upbeat. It is to get the patient talking, it is to stay in the game, even when all you want to do is curl up and sleep!

My sales technique goes like this – I think of the word WELM. It reminds me to ask the patient certain questions. It keeps me in the room, alert and switched on. It gets the patient talking about their feelings, their past and the reasons that drove them to your door. The questions encourage the patient to explore the emotional reasons they arrived at your door. It isn't a cheap sales trick. It starts conversations and allows you to build rapport and take better and more concise clinical notes. It does help you connect with the patient. In truth, it allows you to see the reasons behind the purchase. The real reasons why the patient is sitting in front of you. On many occasions I have found that the patient is in fact unsuitable for treatment. And that is being professional, kind and caring.

W – Why do they **w**ant the treatment?
E – What **E**motion do they attach to the treatment?

L – How **L**ong have they wanted the treatment for?
M – What does it **M**ean to them?

This gets under the bonnet and the patient will appreciate your interest in them. It creates a trusting customer-care relationship. Look, this may not resonate with you but make one up yourself. The final tip: I then use the five points receptionists have recorded whilst on the telephone with them when they booked the appointment. I read them back to the patient. The patients can sometimes get quite overwhelmed. They feel the practice is almost psychic. They sit there wondering how I know they have a blue dog called Chippy, they love Cornwall etc.

So, there we have it. Easily transferable skills. I always told the staff that picked up the phone they had to ask five things. If they couldn't do that, they were not to pick up the phone. We all know we hate answerphones so make sure you have enough staff or use one of those crappy call centres. They are all OK and better than the answerphone, but nothing beats the staff you have trained in your way. If I had my time again the phones would be off the front desk and in the back room where they belong. However, above all, make sure that you are kind and courteous at all times and just try to see it through their eyes, feel how they are feeling. If you learn to do that then anything is possible!

Charles Darwin once said it isn't the strongest of the species that survives nor the most intelligent but those adaptive to change. I firmly believe in this statement. It is also bloody hard to change and takes great courage. When I run courses, I am asked about easy practical advice to improve customer care. It is a regular question. This is my response.

The seller needs to look through the eyes of the purchaser, see how they see it, feel how they feel it, discover why they want to buy. If you achieve this, then anything is possible.

Grant McAree, 2021

I used to sit in my packed waiting room next to all the patients. I listened to the sounds of the business. How nurses called patients, how the TV sounded, how the magazines were placed, how full the bins were. I went for treatment with the dentists and phoned up the business pretending to be a patient. The first step to establishing good customer care is to work out what is failing. Open your eyes and look up from the mouth you are treating. Ask yourself if you would let the business treat your son, daughter, wife or parent. You have to be honest with yourself – where the customer care is failing, where it can do better. When you know, that is half the battle.

Within the dental profession it is usually customer care that falls down and ruins a business. The dentists are too busy playing with all their new gadgets: the latest itero scanner, milling machine or anything else that keeps them occupied when not drilling and filling. That is by no means a criticism. It is a bloody tough job and all you need is to be hand holding staff and teaching them to be kind and courteous. Unfortunately, it is annoying but it is also crucially important to show them you are in charge, this is what you expect and this is how you want it carried out.

How do you work out if you are failing? How do you work out if you need to sharpen up? The ugly truth is that many dentists do not want to know. I didn't want to know, when I started out. I worried about the fallout if I discovered the front of house was crap. The fear of having to discipline, to get rid of, to train etc. all weighs a dentist down and can make them reluctant to even start the process. The process disrupts the day. But if you are brave enough to face it, and really want to develop, just going through this process will put you in the top tier of dentists.

Would you believe me if I told you that most dentists I meet know their receptionists are crap but don't have either the time or the inclination to change it? Or the strength! Like I said, it takes a huge amount of energy to change the hearts and minds of those scary receptionists who have been there for decades before you came on the scene. You, unfortunately, thanks to TUPE regs, had to keep their sorry asses after the purchase! (TUPE regulations are there to protect staff from being fired on day 1 for no other reason than you just want a fresh start with new smiley faces! Follow the law, make sure you understand everyone's rights (including yours). If you do not know them or, like me, can't be bothered to read them, get someone in that knows better and will keep you out of trouble.)

I assume you're ready to step up and that starts with wanting to know what's going on and how to improve. Let us pretend that we want that business that has a price tag in the millions. Because the truth of it, when purchasers and even corporates make offers on your businesses, they will phone up, they will investigate how good your customer care is. In the short term it will also increase the turnover and increase the profit and EBITDA, which in turn will increase the value further. So how do you discover if you have a positive customer care culture?

There are four ways to find out!

1. **What does the owner(you) think?** You can either phone the business up yourself, get a mate or employ someone to record the conversation. Recording calls is not illegal. In fact, at one point I added them to the practice policy and procedures. We advised all staff we would record certain calls and share them with third parties for training and feedback. It is just one way to find out how cringeworthy your reception team really are. And will they fail? Yep, every time. Well, all mine did when I started carrying out this process!

2. **What do patients think?** Send out emails requesting feedback. I have to say I have learnt a lot from Portman. They send emails to every single patient that crosses the threshold. They get feedback and then use the words in the feedback to create a document that can then be formulated into a percentage. Buzzwords. They compare positive words to negative. How clever is that!? Most dental software has reporting capabilities to ensure all patients can be transferred to a list for you to email. You can ask whatever questions make sense for your practice, but I'd advise asking specifically about how they found their treatment and how they found the customer service. Don't put words in their mouth – instead, let them describe the experience.

3. **What do staff think?** This is a toughy. As we have mentioned previously, these are 360 degree feedback exercises and they are scary, especially if your team aren't getting on very well, or you have any disgruntled employees. I used to carry these out anonymously. The main thing is they gave

valuable feedback about the way they felt the customer care could be improved and noticed the poor performers within the team.

4. **What do companies think about you as a client?** This is great. Ask the labs, the bin men, the cleaner – see it from their eyes and ask them for feedback. I learned some very interesting things over the years from this exercise.

But mark my words, it takes courage. It takes true grit to request feedback: 'Don't ask if you don't want to hear!' But be wary of the critique. You know the type. You ask if you look fat in an outfit and they say, 'Yes, very.' They use the truth like a blunt weapon. Do not ignore any advice given, but look at the advice with an adult eye and not that of a wounded child. Keep an eye out for any themes or repeated comments as they will be a good place to start. Some advice is simply not worth actioning, but the quiet ones, the members of staff who prefer to sit in the shadows – the ones who sit at the back watching – they usually are the people who can give so much but rarely do. In a meeting, always watch the quiet ones!

Exercise

I decided one morning I was going to discover the truth. How good were my members of staff? How did the public feel about my business? Would my staff make the five-star hotel grade or were they GP grade? I set out to discover the truth. The whole truth and nothing but The Ugly Truth. This is what you could (and should) try if you have the courage. After all, it does take a great deal of courage because it will then mean that you'll need to act upon both the negative and positive results.

Stage 1
Ask a friend to phone up the surgery on three separate occasions and fill out the Mystery Shop form found in the Resource Pack. Analyse the results. It is pretty self-explanatory.

Stage 2
Ask a friend to visit local coffee shops and ask if there are any good dentists in the area. The second question will be whether there are any bad dentists to avoid. Analyse the results.

Stage 3
Discuss the results with your staff and allow them to offer their thoughts and visions. I always remove names from any feedback. The reasons for this are that the owner of the business is responsible for steering the ship. They need to take full responsibility for the results and not any particular member of staff.

Stage 4
Make changes that were suggested by the members of staff.

Stage 5
Repeat the exercise in six months. I always suggested to members of staff that this was going to happen. It became a bit of a game when the reception team tried to guess who the mystery shopper was if they experienced a difficult caller.

Good luck! As a process, it is some eye opener.

Summary

So, in short:

1. Keep the changes simple.

2. Make sure the changes are transferable so it can be passed to new members of staff.

3. Don't provide scripts – they are boring and usually binned.

4. See through the customers' eyes.

5. Recognise how vital it is to have a tip-top customer care. Especially as the recession looms! Patients will be shopping around.

6. Remember that it is free to have a good customer care.

7. Customer care is a form of marketing – probably the most powerful.

8. Customers are human, so they deserve to be treated with respect.

Go and sit in your waiting room, phone up the business and make an enquiry, get a filling done by the dentist who gets a few complaints. Work out what the issues are and get to work fixing them! I dare you to do a mystery shop, filling out one of the mystery shop forms in the Resource Pack. See what level of service you are providing the public. See if you can do better. Good luck! And remember to be honest.

When you see the results, make those changes but hold on tight! That moody receptionist or over-sensitive nurse will be waiting for you like a caged lion. Use all the techniques in this book, be kind and listen. If that doesn't work, get the big guns in, get lawyered up and manage their ass out of there.

CHAPTER 9

FINANCIAL

My story

Oh dear lord, I could write an entire book about the Finance branch of the tree! Let's be honest, a large majority of dentists choose the profession because it is well paid (one of the reasons, anyway. Who would put up with it if it wasn't!). I remember looking at the university prospectus, and it said (and I will never forget it) that dentistry is a profession that pays well above the average job. Job done, that sounded like the perfect job for me.

What I failed to appreciate when I started out was that the financial branch of the STFD business model was crucial if you wanted to start your own business. I literally had no clue. Safe to say, I bloody winged it! How I survived I do not know. Remembering back to when I opened my first squat practice, I couldn't even cash up. 'WTF? How did I survive those early years?' I will never be able to answer that question. I should have failed financially and emotionally.

So, it began. One year out of my VT training, I found a building. Five-bedroom house. I just knew the area and the building was perfect. Needless to say, I did sod all market research. I put in an offer, as I was so excited about the building and I knew I had found 'the one'. The offer was accepted. I never thought any further about planning. I witnessed my mum and dad building a squat practice. I had seen mates survive; jumping in with two feet was always my pattern of behaviour – still is.

Right, what next? Let's get the bloke who used to fix the dental equipment at the dental practice I was presently working in as an associate: 'BeaverDent'. The same name as my boat (sort of) – *The Wet Beaver* – so it was a sign! They came out to look. They provided a quote. I accepted. I went to the bank. Looking back, maybe it was a bit backwards going to the bank last, but so what? Those bank managers are all out to get me. I deserve the loan; I am unstoppable and invincible, for that matter.

He was a lovely bloke, the NatWest manager called Mark. He asked me for a projection. What the hell was that? So, I asked my accountant. He asked me what I wanted to include in the projection. I didn't bloody know. I just wanted a graph with the line going upwards so the bank would lend me the dollar. So, he drew a graph and I sent it to the bank demanding a 1% above base loan. I got the loan, bought the property and I went to work thinking about marketing the business.

I spent the next six months shitting myself. Therapy, sleepless nights. In truth, I didn't have a bloody clue about how to organise my finances! I was about to start my life. A business owner. I remember day one as I was walking up the road with not a patient in sight. *Oh dear lord, what have I done?* I said to myself.

My manager – another character who I miss very much – spent the next ten years reassuring me. 'It will be fine', she said. And it was. Queuing up patients, money rolling in. Back then I thought to myself, *If I take £400 a day over the desk then I should be fine.* Looking back, where the hell did I get that figure from? It was a total figment of my imagination. Plucked out of the sky. What the hell was I doing? I hadn't calculated costs, expenses, yet I used it as a benchmark. When another associate arrived, all I did was double it! What an absolute bloody tool I was. Don't get me wrong – I had one of the fastest growing private practices in Devon. A super squat. It grew to eight surgeries over a four-year period, all run by an owner who knew sweet FA about business. The Finance branch of my tree had fallen off. To add insult to injury, I was walking along a very expensive road one day and turned to my wife. What I should have done was say, 'Let's sell up.' Instead, I said, 'Let's build another. This practice building game is a piece of cake.' So, we did it again, making all the same mistakes, but I didn't care at the time. I had the passion to acquire. I was building and building fast! If Facebook was around, I would have been posting my success everywhere!

I was a stingy git with materials. I had about ten associates at one stage. I was stingy with equipment as I had no clue about the costs and how it impacted on my business. I accepted that an associate grossing £2k a month was an underachiever, but not as something that needed to be addressed. Staff wages became inflated and I couldn't be bothered to advertise.

I was a 29-year-old millionaire. I remember I left home when I was 26. Waving back to my parents, I shouted back from my clapped-out Mini Metro. I was off to make my million. I had done it. I had achieved my objective. Why should I sweat the small stuff like finances? Bloody hell, I wish I had taken notice of all the small stuff. I tell no word of a lie – the only temperature gauge of a good financial month was that I had more dosh in the account than the same day in the previous month.

I had sleepless nights, shaking, nightmares, sweats, palpitations, depression, anxiety, intrusive thoughts. But I thought I was living the life I dreamed of. I made £50k a month profit at 30 years of age. I couldn't spend my money fast enough (well, not every month). I was a victim of my own poorly thought-out financial planning success. I had the lumpiest pay packets. One minute I was down the Porsche garage, the next I would be on the phone to my dad worried I was going bust. How stressful is that on your soul?

One day I realised I had to change. In the words of Jerry Maguire: 'Breakdown? No, breakthrough.'

This chapter we will discuss the Financial branch of the STFD business model. This branch is non-linear. Of course, the financial aspects of your business are a part of the tree and, therefore, connected to the other branches. Customer service (staff training costs), people (staff wages), websites (maintenance costs), operational (system and training costs).

The financial arm encompasses everything!

You may all be at different stages of the journey. You may be ready to buy into a business, you might want to buy a practice lock, stock and throw out the old vendor, you may be ready to develop and build a squat practice, but the one ugly truth is that you have to get the finances right. The STFD financial branch covers all stages of that journey. It defines what is and isn't a successful business. It isn't only about being cash rich; it is about being richer more easily and with less stress! The word rich is a crude term when only related to money. What I mean is the richness of life. Unfortunately, that means earning money to allow you the pleasantries in life you so deserve, especially if you manage to survive in this crazy world of dentistry. So here is the ugly truth: this is all about that dirty little word that we are all ashamed to speak about, the ugly truth of how it relates to the business of dentistry. Let's talk about money!

Why are finances so important for dentists wanting to grow?

It keeps the wolves from the door

It is why we go to work. Death and taxes. They're the two certainties in life! You need to earn enough to pay for all those cars some dentists like to plaster all over the internet. As dentists, we're used to a lot of disposable income very early on in a career, which leads to expensive outgoings, like the private schools your children go to. Money buys the clothes you wear and the parties you organise. It makes the world go round. So please do not say money isn't important to you. I am not saying you have the passion to acquire and it is the highest on the list, but to wipe it away like it is an irritating fly means you either have too much of it or you are irresponsible. If you got an unfortunate GDC investigation and subsequently lost your job, it is the loss of income that would hit you first: 'How will

I feed my family?' That is the number one stressor. So, it is important to appreciate we all need money; we go to work to earn it, and when we enjoy our job the taste of success is that much sweeter. Earn the money, pay your debts, pay your loans, pay the labs you use and having the funds to do so will make your life that bit more enjoyable and less stressful.

The nature of the beast

Oh my goodness, dentistry is so lumpy. An expression I heard from a finance expert! Basically, it means that one minute you could be loaded and the next broke. I remember going home some months thinking my profit would be sky high. I was left regularly scratching my head wondering how I had done so badly. Bills came in at the wrong time, taxes were due, lab fees were inconsistent. It is a bloody stressful job, so try to control the financial factors that are your responsibility. The financial rollercoaster ride is a bloody killer.

Large range of costs and items we need to buy to service a dental practice

Juggling the financial aspect of a dental practice is difficult because there are just so many things that we need to buy and keep updated and maintained to ensure we're not caught short. We can't give a local anaesthetic and then discover we haven't got enough filling material. We cut a gum open to find we haven't got sutures to close it. Daily spend on materials can fluctuate: it may be a £30,000 chair or £2 of filling material. Maintenance costs can spiral if you don't keep that chair well oiled. Then there is nothing more embarrassing than starting an implant and having to abandon the procedure because you can't recline the chair. All of these costs are often not factored in and can blindside you on a Monday morning, plus you have loss of earnings whilst you are waiting for things to be fixed.

Far too many dentists live in and out of their business overdraft

Due to the lumpy cashflow and the large one-off costs that can come out of the blue, dentists can easily find themselves dipping into their overdraft just to pay the bills. It's really stressful not knowing from month to month whether you're going to buy a Porsche or join the dole queue. Welcome to the game of dentistry.

An increase in goodwill value

The total sale value for all my dental surgeries came to about £5 million. This was only possible after I discovered the importance of ensuring the finance arm of the business was securely understood and developed. As the finances were analysed and a plan developed, the EBITDA improved, profits went up and the value of the business skyrocketed. Remember, small changes across the board can mean massive differences!

You will have more time to enjoy the job

As the profits go up, you can then treat yourself to the fancy equipment that, in turn, leads to further increase in turnover and profit. If everything is a financial mess a new bit of fancy kit will just make further cash flow problems more dire. Above all, you will enjoy the job again. You can put your head down and feel relaxed in the knowledge the business is doing well. Your treatment plans will not be financially motivated. There is nothing more satisfying than turning away a patient who is a red flag, no matter how big their treatment plan is. The desperate approach to treatment goes out the window and you can treat who you like the way you like!

The future

Get ready, it is coming. The perfect storm. Have we forgotten about Brexit? All the other nightmares have covered it up, but the effect has not hit us yet. The war in Ukraine, Covid, tax rises, petrol prices, inflation, interest rate rises – the list goes on. They will all come together. And when they do, the patients who come to see you will not be so easy with their cash. So much money has been pumped into the system with Covid, but it needs to be repaid! In short, many of us will be screwed!

Staff shortages

How many thousands left the profession last year? Are you surprised? And with this shortage what happens? Yep, they demand more money for the jobs they are doing. Just before I sold my last squat practice, I started to recognise costs. I turned to the nurse trainee market. Cheap labour and amazing nurses, but you don't always get lucky with trainees. They may drop in, get trained up and bugger off to the competition. A risky bet! Sometimes that risk pays off.

Coupled with the fact that there are so many patients with so much money just now, there is an increased demand for associates. The result was that the associates wanted greater percentages, better working conditions and more money for less work! Beware of the future – financial planning is key.

Ease the blow by filling the holes in your financial bucket. Plan now rather than sticking a plaster on it later! But to all you associates who think you are in great demand – in the coming months there will be a massive shift. The principals will be back interviewing you and not the other way round.

Future growth and scaling up

If you are not well organised in the finance department, you can get away with it when you are a single-handed dentist. Trust me, I have been there as well! If you order the wrong material or it goes out of date – it has little by way of implications. You will control the number of gloves you use as you have this internal gauge on how many you are using. Every time you reach for another set in the middle of a patient you have this internal dialogue. But as soon as you start expanding, associates are less worried about your bank balance and more worried about their comfort. They won't pick the alginate off their gloves to carry on working. They will just reach for another pair! They won't squeeze out the last bit of acid etch or composite before starting a new batch. You will be considered stingy by everyone. The associates will think you are loaded. They will see their 50% that they give you as their right to run right over you and cost you thousands in wasted materials! I am not saying everyone, but over the years of employing many associates, and being one myself, no one will look after your pocket like yourself.

So, if you plan to expand, get your financial affairs in order before the expansion costs you a fortune. In truth, think about the dentist who had ten practices that could have been just as

---

Ease the blow by filling the holes in your financial bucket. Plan now rather than sticking a plaster on it later!

---

well off if they were on their own cracking out the Invisalign and Implants. Yet the other 30 associates just added to their headache and stress. I want to be clear that associates are not bad! They are just human. They need guidance and to be aware that you are not an open cheque book. Corporates are particularly good at keeping the finances well analysed! The ugly truth is that most associates earn more than their principals.

So, in short and to summarise, why should it be important for dentists to get the finances right? Why should they get the finance branch of the STFD business model finely tuned? The answer is it is important for any business to get it right to be the best they can be. For dentists, avoid that lumpy cash flow problem that is so common in the dental world. Try to create some calm, avoiding that end of month sinking feeling when you get presented with that dreaded list. It's the list that shows you how much you have to pay associates. In truth, I resented that list. In the early days, some of them were routinely earning more than me and had the cheek to tell me how to run my business. Ungrateful pillocks? Nah, I just managed my finances badly.

Client Story: The Power of Accountability

A dentist from the Midlands rang me as we emerged from the Covid nightmare. In her opinion she was not earning enough money. In truth, she was disappointed and expected to be earning more since she had been in the game long enough. She had seen a number of dentists buying Ferraris and Porches and posting them online. Incidentally, a number of those dentists had posted their houses with their cars in the driveway. The price of the cars seemed more expensive than the house! I don't get that mentality! I did point this out to her and that immediately lifted her spirits. People will only post what they want you to see. They will never post the bits in their lives that are bad. I have made it my goal never to post about my relationship. Not even on my anniversary. My wife is my life and I am the only one who needs to know that. Well, and my wife of course!

Anyway, we are all motivated by different things. We can all sit back and reflect on life; we can assess what we have and decide if it is enough. When is it enough? For me, it is never enough. With my family I am 100% satisfied. I am a lucky man. However, with my business I am never satisfied.

This dentist, who will remain anonymous, was the same. She just felt totally unsatisfied with her business. Family – great. Business – the pits. There was a deep-seated feeling of resentment, though. She was paying staff too much, associates that either earnt too much – this meant that they were earning more than the dentist in question (the principal!) – or associates that were not earning enough and moaned about not getting enough new patients to sustain a good income. When approached about the turnover the associate became defensive and dismissive using the 'I am self-employed' card and then proceeded to criticise reception, saying they were sending rubbish leads. 'Rubbish leads', like I have said is a term that really annoys me. There's no such thing as poor leads, just poor conversion and sales techniques. I blame the teachers and mentors who use this terminology.

The following were the dentist's list of complaints in no particular order:

1. She was not earning enough (practice profit was lower than expected).

2. Associates were not consistent with earnings.

3. There was a spiralling amount of bad debt within the surgery.

4. Some dentists were being favoured with regard to new patients (a common one).

5. The rubbish dentists were getting more new patients, as their books were always empty!

6. Dentists weren't confident and were selling the cheaper treatments.

7. Materials bills were too high.

8. Laboratory costs were spiralling.

9. She wanted to dump the NHS and earn more money.

10. She wasn't sure whether the practice was doing well or not.

You may look at this list and sympathise with the dentist. I know I have experienced all of these issues over time. I said I had an associate that earnt so little it was better to ask them not to turn up to work as I would make more of a profit. I have had associates moan about poor leads. I've also experienced spiralling debts, once getting a loan to help pay for my tax!

When that happens, it is a bloody slippery slope. This is where this dentist was heading.

Assessment, diagnosis and planning. I treat problems like an orthodontic patient. The primary problem was a complete lack of systems in place to analyse what was going on with the finances. There were no reports, and all the issues were based on feelings and not hard facts. Staff ruled the roost and knee-jerk reactions were commonplace. Because there was no way to assess the situation properly, she had nothing to diagnose and then couldn't plan to make improvements. Decisions were not based on facts; money was spent on expensive marketing firms in an attempt to fill the bucket with more water. They produced results but that didn't bear fruit as it wasn't the issue that needed changing. Reception training had been carried out and forgotten. The staff had been replaced and the systems that had been put in place had not been carried forward to the new members of the team.

Please reader – stop throwing money at a problem till you know what the problem is.

The dentist was broken. The stress was immeasurable. I have been there. I have been alone in bed shaking with fear. I once went to the GP as I thought I had MS. I had an uncontrollable tingling. They tested me for that, but it came back negative – so I went to another specialist as I was then convinced I had MND. The same was happening to this lovely broken dentist. The tingling was down to anxiety. A lack of oxygen due to stress! I referred the dentist for stress management and therapy. The dentist had lost total control of the business. It had gone on too long and she felt so torn between selling the business and soldiering on! Or, of course, just shutting the door and walking away.

The staff wanted more money. They wanted more money as they were feeling the stress too. The customer care was poor and the finances were suffering because of that. The entire business was going down the pan at a rate of knots. It was a sinking ship full of angry staff members ready to jump ship and join a happier crew down the road!

What did I do/advise?

Whenever I speak to dentists who feel broken, I always start with normalising the situation. If we find ourselves in a stressful situation, we always blame ourselves. That is normal. It is also normal to find yourself on the edge. It is human nature. Over my career I have faced all sorts of personal and business challenges. I call them challenges, as I have always got through them. I have come back from being broken many times. That is part of the human experience. So, normalising the way she was feeling instantly gave her a lift.

We then agreed on a way forward. We would assess, diagnose and make a plan. I said that at the end, if the plan was to sell the business, so be it. In my experience, never corner anyone. Always give them a way out. Give choice! Part of my USP! I feel so much compassion for dentists who are struggling – if you have been there and done it, worn the t-shirt, you can appreciate the pain that one can feel when depression and anxiety get a grip. The feeling that you have to go to work and carry on. But with my experience of this and the experience of crawling back, I inspired the dentist to find a plan!

The first action was to diagnose. We agreed there was a problem. Some of the appointment books were rammed full whilst other clinicians had massive gaps. There were spiralling bad debts, the takings were lumpy and the profit was poor. All of the information can be found in the reports section of the SOE software. The problem was they were not using the reports available to them.

We added the RoboReception ChatBot to the website, we introduced the CRM system (RoboReception LeadTracker). Go to the *Resource Pack: Task 11*. There you'll find a video showing you how to create your own CRM.

Getting people to buy in was the tough bit. When there is a negative feeling there's a blame culture, so the best thing to do in this situation is to create an accountability culture. Each to their own. They become responsible for the jobs they were employed to do, and they also become aware this can then be measured. It can also be measured by everyone else. When you can measure performance, the blame culture diminishes.

Finally, everyone was accountable. There was no place to hide. I then taught the reception how to ask for money. Remember, the Customer Care branch of the STFD Business Model! The staff were to ask for half or all of the fees for the next appointment, providing choice. Suddenly, bad debt was a thing of the past. The practice was getting fees up front.

The Lead Management Board could then show who got what and where. It showed which dentists were being provided with new patients and who managed to convert treatments, from reception to dentists. It just showed where the cracks were. Suddenly, when everyone could see, the cracks got filled.

The initial result was staggering. Bad debt improved, cash flow increased, staff felt more in control. The dentists suddenly stepped up their game, as they felt like they were accountable. They knew it was no longer a 'free-for-all' system. It was a system based on fact and any complaints could be answered effectively and a plan could be then put in place.

My client was over the moon. She no longer felt lost. I always feel humans buckle when they experience a lack of power. I am not talking about power-hungry plonkers. I mean a total lack of power. Humans need to be in control in a small way and if that is taken away a feeling of fear sets in. My client had that power back. She had direction and she had a purpose again.

I have to say, when I need to relax after a hard day I like to think of sparkle moments. These are moments in my life I am particularly proud of. This is one of them. It gives me a warm feeling that all that suffering I went through can be put to good use. It was all worth it. I have another sparkle moment. It is writing this book and sharing all the knowledge I have gained over a very long and interesting career. Stuff that has happened to me and experiences I have endured makes me the person I am today. If I can share that and help make others have a little less of a bumpy ride, like this dentist, what a sparkle that is!

How to improve your finance

Step 1: Recognise and accept

This is the toughest yet easiest! This may not make sense to you, but it will. I remember I used to go to therapy and have an issue. It could be anything. Struggling with my feelings, falling in love, you name it; I was screwed up. My therapist always said the same thing. It starts by me admitting I had a problem that I wanted to change. So true – we need to be honest with ourselves. So, ask yourself these questions and be really honest about your answers.

- Is the business where I want it to be?

- Am I earning enough?

- Is the business working to its full potential?

- Do I feel financially stable?

- Do I resent any associates for not earning enough?

- Do I resent some associates for wanting more time with appointments?

- Do I resent certain associates for asking for more equipment/materials?

- Do I have enough money to pay my taxes?

- Did I make a mistake opening or buying the business?

- Would I have been better off as an associate?

- Am I always in an overdraft?

- Do I make nothing some months?

Step 2: Assessment (hourly rate)

The best place to start is working out your hourly rate. A simple method. A bit of fun. Or it may make you s*** yourself. This will tell you how much you have to earn per clinic! Finding out the hourly clinic rate can be a tricky calculation to predict. Please see the exercise below.

And remember to incorporate a CRM system like the one Donna and I have developed, the RoboReception LeadTracker. It gives all sorts of information for you to assess. It allows you to get under the bonnet. Discover who is not pulling their weight and where the chain is broken.

Step 3: Diagnosis (recognising who are the poor associates)

The questions have been answered, and some may resonate with you. Others may not. Resonate – that is a funny word. What I mean is when you read some of the questions you sit thinking to yourself, *Oh bloody hell, that is me*.

• Is the business where I want it to be?

That is quite a generic question that can cover all sorts of aspects of your business. I regularly asked myself how I was feeling, still do. I call it checking in! If it is a feeling I can't put my finger on, I go to a therapist. See if the reasons for my awkward feelings have a place. That is the problem with the mind – you can't walk through all the doors and just find what you are looking for. Sometimes it takes time.

When I was developing my first business, I got quite anxious. I discovered it was a feeling of excitement. I was just forgetting to breathe – so make sure you do not rush, have some alone time to discover what the feeling is. Really look inside yourself to find the cause of your negativity. It may not always be negative. If you are clear about where your business is heading and you know it is definitely not where you want it to be, you need to go back to discovering your passion and uniqueness. Is the business going in the direction you want it to? Are you trying to grow a massive industry when you have no passion to acquire?

• **Am I earning enough?**

Always separate entitlement and what you need. Many dentists feel they should earn a certain amount if they are a business owner or if they do implants. They see social media posts that may indicate that certain dentists have great wealth. I promise you that 99% are false appearances set by dentists who are determined to have an image rather than post reality. I have clients who are nearly broke yet appear to be living a good life.

Make sure you have enough for you and yours, make sure you are sensible, make sure you are not going deeper into an overdraft every month. If the graph is going upwards and you are earning enough to live, you are doing fine. And to be honest – when is it ever enough? We will live just within our means (well, the sensible ones do), so this feeling is certainly not uncommon.

If you find you are going deeper and deeper into your overdraft, you may find the practice needs help. The first person to speak to is the bank. They are not there to close you down. If you wait for them to contact you, then it is a very different discussion. They can tailor loans, reduce monthly payments, provide support and advice.

• **Is the business working to its full potential?**

I don't know a business that works to its full potential 100%, but there is nothing worse than wasted talent. In any business or industry. If you feel this is your resonating question, you probably see the phone ringing too much and the staff can't cope, or the phone not ringing enough and the eager staff are left waiting to greet the callers with their amazing skills. It will be an either/or. If it rings too much you need to get the phones off the desk and into the back room. The staff are clearly overworked so get more staff in. It is always better to be overstaffed than understaffed! Always! If the phone isn't ringing, then get the marketing spruced up! Study the patient journey and see where it is going wrong. Go back to your USP. Are you carrying out the dentistry you want to be doing? Full potential is only reached when you feel fulfilled. You will only be fulfilled if you love doing what you do.

- **Do I feel financially stable?**

If I was to be brutally honest, I do not think I have felt a moment of financial peace since I started my own business. It could have been the GDC, the CQC, the defence organisations – over the last ten years I have been anxious about my job being taken away from me. Everything could come crashing down. So, this is the question that resonates with me. This is my fear. The only way I have helped myself is to build and pay off loans, become less dependent on the banks, on me working. I have grown the business to rely less and less on my income. If your business is solely reliant on you, this fear will stay with you until your retirement.

- **Do I resent any associates for not earning enough?**

Either the associates earn too much or too little. Some months I went home with less than my associates and I held such resentment. I took the risks, I had the loans, I carried the can. And now we have non-delegable duty. Reality check – owning a practice is ten times more stressful than being an associate. Please respect your principal. I would look out of the window at the end of the day, watching the associates skip down the road. They may have a gross of £8k for the month. So, they took home about £3,000. I had bills to pay. They were off on holiday. They didn't seem to care, but my question to you is this: why should they care? They didn't choose to take on the stresses you have as an owner. So, if they earn too much or too little, either train the underachiever to do better and risk losing them or don't wind yourself up. Remember the low grosser will still be adding to the goodwill of the business. Over the years I have found the big grossers got more complaints, and gave me a bigger headache, but this is just my experience.

- **Do I resent certain associates for asking for more equipment/materials?**

If you feel that the business is not doing well financially, the natural reaction is to tighten the purse strings. In tough times, I would moan at the number of gloves, the waste of certain materials. Were the nurses squeezing out the last bits of composites? This just added to the stress. My advice is to make sure everyone is accountable. Make sure clinics can be assessed. If they are using too many composites then the dentist can be approached. Preferably by the manager and not the owner. A good manager will conduct a money chat with less charged feelings. The conversation is then more positive and goals can be discussed, rather than the conversation going south. I remember I used to try to approach the 'saving materials' chat with a couple of associates on a number of occasions. It never ended well! I remember I fell out with an associate as I snapped, 'You don't earn enough to take all the time off. Hey, here is a fiver – don't come in tomorrow as I will be better off!' I felt awful.

- **Do I resent some associates for wanting more time for appointments?**

When the business is doing financially well, requests for longer appointments are welcomed. You can get that warm fuzzy feeling. The associates are wanting to improve on their sales and customer care. However, if the patient numbers are reducing and the associates are performing poorly, the voices in my head are always, 'You lazy plonker – go and start your own business and stop playing around.' I always let my manager deal with these sensitive requests, finding out why the associate wants more time. Remember, they get stressed as well. Dentistry is a difficult job and you don't have to be an owner to break under the pressure. A happy stress-free associate is a more productive one. Take them out to dinner, find out what is going on in their lives. I was guilty of not doing this over the years.

- **Do I have enough money to pay my taxes?**

This is the crux of it. Do you have enough to pay your taxes? You earn a certain amount and have to pay tax on that amount. So, either you have a bloody awful accountant or you are not taking care of your business finances. If you get to tax time and you need to get a loan or go deeper into an overdraft, the accountant is the second person to discuss this with. Then you need to be seriously looking at what you spend your money on. Is it fast cars? Maybe big houses you cannot afford? Private school fees? Are you taking too much out of the business?

- **Did I make a mistake opening or buying the business?**

Every time I went through a difficult time, I asked this question. Is it just self-doubt? It is part of human nature, but ignore this pressing doubt. Let it drive you to do better. In four weeks' time you may well be back up on top and off to buy your dream car. Sometimes it is good to get a dental mentor/coach to discuss these thoughts with. I had a client who rang me up monthly. It was always a quick call: 'I am screwed', 'I am going bust', 'Am I earning enough?' All those negative thoughts. As soon as they were aired, they felt better and went back to work. They are now opening their fourth squat practice.

- **Would I have been better off as an associate?**

If you look at your monthly takings, you may have been better off, less stressed and with less to worry about. Many months you will take home more than the principal, but then you are not in charge. You can't steer the ship your way. You won't have anything to sell at the end of the day. Again, these thoughts come around when things are hard. When business is going great there is no better feeling.

I suppose running a successful business is like a drug: you can get addicted to it. But there is always a come down, a reality check. Looking at associates driving their sports cars and having long holidays does give the owner a bit of a reality check and it can hit quite hard. Best not to follow these thoughts, as they can be quite consuming and damaging to the business.

- **Am I always in an overdraft?**

My advice is if you are in an overdraft, that is fine. If you bounce in and out that is fine. But if you are going deeper and deeper, you really need to contact the bank and discuss a way forward with your accountant. I once took a loan out to pay off another loan and clear my tax bill. I was devastated and realised I had to do something. Then I started to take my finances more seriously!

- **Do I make nothing some months?**

The lumpy pay of a dentist. Do not panic. Some months I went to work, worked my ass off, only to discover I had made nothing. In fact, sometimes I made a negative balance. I had more money in the bank the previous month. They were the toughest months. You just have to dig deep and move on to the next month and plan a little better or accept that it was just a bad month. Review your bills and expenditure; you will probably discover that the month in question would have just been an unlucky month for the accumulation of bills! I used to phone my dad and ask him for advice. I must have done that every few months for 20 years. It was just reassuring to know that all dentists experience these fears.

Step 4: Tips and tricks

Avoid debt by training receptionists to ask for deposits upfront

Be polite and ask if the patient wants to pay for half or all of their next appointment.

Stop offering interest-free loans

Who on earth would agree to using this awful method of sales? It can be 10% off the top profit paying their interest. Patients always ask first, 'Can you pay monthly?' That is their primary concern. Drop this interest-free rubbish! When they ask if it is interest free, make sure you have an answer!

Make sure your team know the numbers to focus on

Would you believe me if I told you that for 25 years I never failed to ask my staff how many new patients booked in and what the gross takings were for the day? I didn't give a damn about the answer. If it was poor, I never told them off. If it was good, I always congratulated them. Why? I wanted my staff to think these two factors were the most important numbers in the business. New patients and turnover. Subconsciously, it makes them work harder to achieve a good result, so the owner could congratulate them if the numbers were good.

Have some money set aside for a rainy day

I always made sure I had £100k in the business account for a rainy day. It just gave me reassurance. What is your number? Most of us have one!

Get on top of your inventory

Just before I sold my last squat, I had designed a system whereby everyone had to sign out everything. Gloves, bibs. I was about to go one step further. I was about to create accounts for each clinical room (Henry Schein etc.)! Everyone in my building was going to be accountable for everything they ordered. Right down to matrix strips. Nothing would go unnoticed. Accountability is key. Too controlling? I don't give a damn. Go run your own practice if you don't like it. Live in my shoes for a day because I promise you this – I have worked on both sides of the fence and returning to being an associate in my last ten years of dentistry was a breeze in comparison.

The stresses of ownership wore me down more than I realised. Get your finances spot on and ease that burden. Funny thing is we hate corporate dentistry, but Portman has this area covered; they can assess, diagnose and plan the ins and outs of a duck's arse. They are fantastic at it. The reason a lot of dentists don't like corporate companies is down to this. The corporates know what to look for, they know how to make changes and they will do so without feeling, which is something we are not used to as a profession. I am finding myself respecting their way. The approach is business-like and sometimes ruthless. I am finding myself assessing my other businesses in this fashion and passing these skills on to my clients. The problem is we were never taught business at dental school! But, then again, neither were my lawyer or my accountant!

Transparent pricing and a range of options

Setting fees is a minefield. If I could advise you one golden tip then it would be to always offer choice. This includes if you are going private. Offer three or four different crown prices: basic (NHS equivalent), independent, superior and deluxe. Offer three or four denture types. Even root treatments. It always worried me that patients would opt for an extraction of a molar due to the price of a root treatment at the back of the mouth. It may take longer to find three canals – but I found patients favoured paying more for a front tooth root treatment than a molar. When I discovered this trend I started charging more for an incisor RCT than a molar. Patients kept their teeth – happier patients! It's about choice, choice and more choice. Patients hate parting with their cash, so monthly payments work – make it as easy as possible for patients to pay you!

Communicate any fee changes in person

Money is a horrible word. If you are planning to change the fees, go private, whatever that change may be, always carry this out face to face – always give the warning in person to soften the blow. Never send letters out. I did this once in my career when I wanted to leave the NHS and transfer all the patients privately. Almost finished me emotionally and professionally. I was gutted and I got some hideous replies. One gentleman said I was greedy, conniving, thoughtless and evil. It went on with insult after insult. So, if you are planning to go private, always test the water, dip your toe in. You could approach one or two patients and see how it lands. You could send a couple of letters out and see if you receive a favourable response. You could also train reception to tell a few chosen clients. When you know which works best, you are ready to let the world know you are about to dump the NHS and rip out their souls! Well, that is how some people feel about our beloved NHS. I ended up on the front page of my local newspaper. They almost had me smoking a cigar on my boat *The Wet Beaver*. It was a hideous article, but I survived! I sold the business for millions in the end, so it didn't end badly.

Don't bundle in services the patient doesn't need

Setting the fees was always important to me. I always managed to put myself in the patient's shoes. I never included anything in the check-up fee. So 'free' included radiographs were never part of my business plan. Why would you even want to do this? My competitor charges £50 for a new patient exam. They include radiographs. I charge £28 for my exam fee. I charge an extra £30 for radiographs. So, my new patient exam fee is more yet I register 200 new patients a month. They register a third of that! It is down to the exam fee. I hear you say, 'Doesn't that upset patients when you advise them that they need radiographs?' That is all in the sales tips and tricks. It is up to them if they want them or not. It is all about choice.

Don't push the sale before the patient is ready

When you get that squeaky bum feeling when you are about to advise the patient the price of the treatment - that feeling is a warning. The patient is not high enough on the purchasing ladder of awareness. If you get that feeling, listen to the warning and don't offer up the price until you know the patient is ready. The only way to ensure they are ready is to ask more questions, build rapport and listen to their pain points, their worries, their needs. I then advise the price but immediately offer them a get out. I let them know they can go to the next stage, whether it is a full assessment or ClinCheck, but they can change their mind at that stage and shouldn't feel pressured. I also offer them a smile guarantee for their money, but I'm unable to offer that promise until a full assessment has been carried out. The money chat then becomes that much easier; the power is in my hands, as I am not ready to sign the patient up until I have the full details required to provide that promise. It is like a game of tennis: it's where the ball sits at the end of the rally that matters. This isn't just dentistry! It is life. Provide choice, provide freedom of choice, no pressure, no sales techniques and just be you. But look through their eyes and you will win every time.

Exercise

So here is a small exercise to help you establish what your costs are. The business expenses. Please don't slit your throat when you discover you earn less than your hairdresser. Remember, it is all in the assessment – diagnosis – plan! Remember, there is always a way to do better. So over to you – let's do this, let's be the best you can be.

Adam Bobby, AMS Medical Accountants, helped me with this. Thanks, pal. I hate this stuff but it is a necessary evil!

1. Income

Desired yearly income – what you would like to earn?
Let us say £100k.

2. Total up all your business expenses. Those are all the things you need to pay for

- marketing

- computer

- website and hosting

- travel

- taxes

- subcontractors

- office supplies

- professional memberships

- training courses

- accounting and bookkeeping fees

- legal advice

- bank charges

- rent

- wages.

Let us say you have calculated it all up over the year and it comes to £150k. This is what is tricky about a squat! You have to guess a bit or ask someone who has been there and done it!

3. Calculate your true cost of being in business

Add your yearly income and your business expenses together.
£250k

So, to make 100k and to pay all your bills you will need to make £250k. So far so good.

4. Calculate your billable hours (hours you will have your head down making money)

You will need to consider:

1. Sick days each year
   e.g. 15 days (3 weeks)

2. Holiday days each year
   e.g. 20 (4 weeks)

3. Bank holiday days each year
   8 days

4. Weekends
   52 x 2 (Sat & Sun) = 104

To get your billable hours you will take away all the above days from 365 to confirm your yearly working days.

365 - 104 - 15 - 20 - 8 = **218** days left to make £250k
You work 7 hours a day. So:
218 x 7 (Hours) = 1,526

5. Hourly clinic rate

£250k divide by 1526 hours = £163.83 – your hourly rate! That is what you need to make per hour every hour. If you fall back one hour you need to make it back up the next.

Whilst this looks easy, it can also be quite daunting. In the Resource Pack I have made a simple spreadsheet. Stick in your numbers and it will give you a general idea of hourly costs.

Summary

I do need to stress that no one is perfect. I remember I asked an amazing person to come in and do a business health check because I had no clue about this stuff – I was building a super squat at the time. This is how I met Lesley Bailey, turned the business upside down and managed to add a third onto the gross before one of my sales. Then I flogged the super squat to a superpowerhouse, known then as IDH. Now – Mydentist.

My point is, no matter how good you are, it is always a benefit to have an outside person come in to give it a fresh eye. It doesn't mean you are failing. You may survive if you don't get it 100% right, but why not make it easier for yourself? So, work out your hourly rate and see if you are behind. Get a great CRM system, see where staff need help, and enjoy a richer life – one with less stress – and do what you were trained to do: dentistry!

Whilst you remember to get the finance branch finely tuned, do not forget about the dentistry. Upskill. Don't open a dental clinic without being able to provide the services you want to sell or the treatments that are in demand. Thanks to Tif Qureshi and Ross Hobson – IAS, I managed to upskill and provide orthodontics properly. Not a weekend course. Coupled with getting the finances right, I managed to do the right treatment, for the right cost, on the right patient. My turnover skyrocketed and increased the value of my business. Remember that small changes everywhere offer massive benefits!

Conclusion

Making a change is worthy of a celebration. That is why we go to therapy, go to university, pick up a book. To make a change. It is to develop and head towards a goal you have made or not quite made consciously. A conscious goal is when we have direction. We can adjust the sails and head towards it. We can have everyone on board who all have the same aspirations or are happy to support you on the journey. You have committed time to reading this book and hopefully carried out the exercises and downloaded the Resource Pack. A simple exercise like calculating your required hourly rate can enable you to structure your entire business. Set your fees, educate and support the right members of your team.

You are now empowered to:

- Fill the holes in your leaking bucket and start putting your money to good use!

- Stop wasting your finances on crap marketing campaigns.

- Discover your USP – the roots to the STFD business model and the core to a successful business.

- Train your team to provide that five-star hotel service.

- Define and map out that patient journey.

- Never lose a patient or forget to send that treatment plan.

- Motivate your team, empowering them to feel they are part of a family.

- Hire better and create an amazing working culture.

- Improve your conversion rate and stay out of trouble. Go to the *Resource Pack: Task 12* Invisalign Treatment notes templates. (An added bonus to help you write amazing notes. The only bit of clinical advice I have offered in the book!)

- Train all staff so that they can confidently sell treatments.

- Get your finances in order so you have no more sleepless nights.

- Calculate your actual costs/rates so you can design not just a financially viable business but a very profitable one.

- Ignore fancy posts as the dentists posting them are probably miserable.

- Create attractive social media posts that cost nothing.

- Analyse your business to see where it is going wrong.

- Create an environment where everyone can be assessed and accountable (including you!).

- Make better decisions about your business.

- Reduce the number of knee-jerk reactions that usually end in tears!

And of course…

Enjoy the job you were trained to do and let the rest take care of itself, effectively and appropriately!

Next steps

It is the end of the chapter, and the end of the book. I feel a bit sad really. I have thoroughly enjoyed cleansing my soul and sharing all my stories and real-life experiences, but it is just the beginning for you. You can get to work tomorrow on all the free tips and tricks. It would also be a pleasure to meet you, be it through a webinar, one of my courses, or 1:1 coaching and mentoring. For now, go to the Resource Pack and make sure you make use of all the freebies!

The future for me

1. **1:1 coaching** in 2023. I am taking on a small group of clients in 2023 and helping them develop the five-star hotel service! It's the ultimate patient journey, where the baton never drops. We will be fully supporting clients and their staff, providing reception training and assisting associates with clinical conversion techniques whilst developing a personalised CRM system that will provide the ultimate analysis and accountability. You will have me there 24/7. Well, apart from when I sleep! Any situations you are unsure about, any problems you are experiencing, a business you want to develop, then I will be there, supporting you every step of the way.

2. **Online course** – How To Create Knock Out Open Days. Online is all the rage. We will be providing group sessions and a 1:1 course for the dentists who are unable to travel. An Open Day is a hugely powerful tool; from opening a squat to promoting treatments, such as dental implants, Invisalign, and general dentistry, it can dictate the pace

of future success. If you've ever been worried about open days then rest assured, I've felt all of the following over the years in the run-up to the event: Will patients turn up? Will anyone turn up? Why haven't my staff supported me on this journey? Have I wasted my money on catering? Do I have to go home with my tail between my legs after all that advertising?

3. But here's the great news: I have some simple tips and tricks to help you smash it! So, let me share my strategy, which works, with you. If there is any other topic you would like me to cover in an online course, drop me a line.

4. **The Squat Course** – This will help you to learn how to locate, develop and build a squat practice. I totally get the fear of starting up from scratch, having done it five times myself. I'll share all of my tips and tricks so you can hit the ground running. They're all the things I wish I'd realised at the time. After this course, you'll either a) be confident in your plans or b) change direction. Either way, it's good to know! I understand the fear, having had many nights lying awake worried. I would have benefitted from an experienced dentist to share those fears. Just to share ideas and plans. From someone who has real experience, my journey would have been more tolerable. This is what I want to do for you. That journey can be great. Those initial hurdles and fears can turn you away from your dreams. That is the tragedy. Let me show you a pathway until you find yours.

5. **The full Dental Business and Marketing Course** – Business Coach For Dentists. Join me for a full day masterclass, typically for groups of 10 to 25 dentists and designed for those wanting more than to just get by. I'll share all of my tips and tricks for marketing and advertising, learnt from the triumphs and failures of countless campaigns and strategies. I'll show you canny ways to save time and money and where to get free advice and management support to fire up your business! You'll also be invited to a WhatsApp group after the event where you can ask questions and get advice if you're unsure about anything.

For more information on any of these options, check out my website: www.dentalbusinessmentor.co.uk

I would love for you to connect with me.

Jump into the Facebook Group – Dental Business and Marketing – to connect with thousands of other dentists and marketers within the industry to share ideas and learn.

https://www.facebook.com/groups/511575225902292

Check out my mentor page for more free tips and tricks:
https://www.facebook.com/DrGrantMcAreeBDS/
Instagram: https://www.instagram.com/dentalbusinessmentor/
Email : grantmcaree@gmail.com
Tel : 07896877827

I would really love it if you could get in touch and tell me about your journey and if any of the book resonated with you. Let me know if you are struggling! A worry shared is a worry halved, after all.

I hope you have enjoyed this book. Enjoyed reading it as much as I have writing it. If you have found it useful, please post about it. Share your journey. It will help others who are struggling to find their way. Gaining knowledge is always the answer to many problems. We will always be faced with challenges – it is part of the human experience – but if we keep learning, and keep sharing – we are stronger together.

Dentistry is a wonderful profession. It can be as much fun as it is crippling. I am privileged to be part of a wonderful community. I will leave you with my line. You know I have to say it, you know it is my signature, so here it is: at 52 years young I have finally realised that all this business of dentistry...

'IT AIN'T ROCKET SCIENCE.'

With Love,
Dr Grant McAree BDS BSc (Hons)

Acknowledgements

Whilst I find myself thinking about who to thank for helping me write this book, my mind keeps drifting back to my family. My wife, my children. To my son, Joshua, my daughter, Mia, and my wife Sarah – you have made my world a better place. To Sarah, who has been my rock, always saying 'what now? Not another project!', yet continuing to support me through all my ups and downs. And to Josh and Mia – you always make me proud in everything you do. Because of you three, I strive to be a better person. From being told at the age of 15 I would never pass my O-level English, to writing a book at 52 – you three make me realise anything is possible.

Printed in Great Britain
by Amazon

40264826R00138